Philosophical and Economic Foundations of Capitalism

Philosophical and Economic Foundations of Capitalism

Edited by
Svetozar Pejovich
Texas A&M University

LexingtonBooks
D.C. Heath and Company
Lexington, Massachusetts
Toronto

Library of Congress Cataloging in Publication Data

Main entry under title:

Philosophical and economic foundations of capitalism.

Papers presented at a conference sponsored by the Liberty Fund, held in Freiburg, Germany, in Feb. 1981.
Includes bibliographical references and index.
1. Capitalism—Congresses. I. Pejovich, Svetozar. II. Liberty Fund.
HB501.P4185   1982   330.12'2   82–48047
ISBN 0–669–05906–4

Copyright © 1983 by D.C. Heath and Company

Published simultaneously in Canada

Printed in the United States of America

International Standard Book Number: 0–669–05906–4

Library of Congress Catalog Card Number: 82–48047

*To Susan, who has been a continual source
of inspiration and encouragement to me*

Contents

Tables

Preface

The Age of Enlightenment, discoveries in the physical sciences (for example, the laws of gravitation and motion), and opportunities for entrepreneurship (new frontiers) caused some important changes in man's conception of the universe and his society. These changes were a direct result of the slow, uneven, but persistent increase in man's understanding that (1) knowledge is power; (2) the wealth of nations is not fixed, but is subject to immense growth; (3) personal ambitions and incentives are the primary driving force in man's pursuit of happiness; and (4) the community is a voluntary association of free individuals, seeking efficient outcome.

A major and predictable consequence of this new age was more focus on the economic side of life. The search for ways to foster ambitions of individuals, to strengthen their personal incentives, to make people vertically and horizontally mobile, and to promote economic growth required the development of new institutions that would be capable of channeling the human race in the direction of orderly and coordinated pursuits of economic gains. Eventually, capitalism and socialism were born. Capitalism appeared first in England and Holland in the early seventeenth century. Socialism remained a product of intellectual thinking until the Soviet revolution in 1917. The capitalist system quickly demonstrated its economic efficiency and spread throughout Western Europe and the North American continent.

According to F.A. von Hayek, capitalism proved to be an effective way of making man take part in a process more complex than he could comprehend since it was through the free market that he contributed to ends that were not part of his purpose. Hayek argued that in the free market "knowledge that is used in it is that of all its members. Ends that it serves are the separate ends of those individuals in all their variety and contrariness. [In socialistic markets] only the knowledge of the organizer can enter into the design of the economy proper, and all members of such an economy . . . must be guided in their actions by the unitary hierarchy of ends which it serves" (F. Hayek, "Competition as a Discovery Procedure," *New Studies in Philosophy, Politics, Economics, and the History of Ideas,* Chicago, University of Chicago Press, 1978, p. 183).

The central problem of our time is that the origins of capitalism, its philosophical foundations, and its morality have been either ignored or misunderstood by the intellectual community. A possible explanation for this absence of critical evaluation of social foundations of capitalism is that modern economic analysis, with its sophisticated techniques, has fostered the view that capitalism is a social system which is exclusively, ruthlessly, and cold bloodedly concerned with one single issue: economic efficiency. Thus, capitalism has been tolerated for its performance but never appreciated for its philosophical and moral quality.

Cognizant of this problem, the Liberty Fund sponsored in February 1981 a conference on "The Philosophical and Economic Foundations of Capitalism." The conference was held in Freiburg, Germany. The purpose of this volume is to make the papers presented at the conference (and subsequently reedited) available to the intellectual community at large. The book's emphasis is on those moral and philosophical qualities of capitalism that have been neglected for too long. The issues covered in the book range from basic institutions of capitalism and socialism (Pejovich) to the origins of capitalism (Hartwell and Opp), the analysis of the morality of capitalism (Koslowski and Buchanan), and critical evaluation of the nature of its social processes (Vanberg); from social incentives to inject elements of socialism into the capitalist system (Hayek) to the analysis of socialist practices in the West (Pejovich and Ståhl).

The range of topics in the book is too broad to have answered all the basic questions concerning social qualities of capitalism. However, I hope that the various chapters will elicit attention and stimulate further research that will explore capitalism as a way of life.

I am grateful to Judy Roessner for her clerical assistance in preparing this manuscript.

1

Basic Institutions of Capitalism and Socialism

Svetozar Pejovich

Capitalism

In Roman law the term *capital* was used to distinguish the principal of a loan from interest and other carrying charges. The term reappeared in the seventeenth century and was used interchangeably with other terms such as *wealth* and *the stock of physical goods*. J. Schumpeter was perhaps the first economist of some influence to define capital as a purely monetary category: Capital is the sum of means of payments which is available at any moment for transference to the entrepreneur.[1] Capital is that specific power which enables the entrepreneur to divert resources from their routine uses. Adam Smith described capitalism—he never used the term *capitalism,* though—as an autonomous, self-generating, self-propelling, and self-regulating system that is capable of producing both the wealth of nations and social harmony.

Institutions of Capitalism

Fundamental institutions of capitalism are the *right of ownership* in productive assets, the *freedom of contract,* and *limited government*. These institutions set capitalism apart from other social systems. They generate specific and predictable behaviors that are consistent with economic efficiency and individual liberty. Private ownership is a powerful and perhaps necessary means for the dispersion of power in a society. Contractual freedom and limited government replace orders from the top by voluntary exchange in open markets. The individual whose behavior is guided by the principles of self-interest, self-responsibility, and self-determination, is then the real decision maker in a capitalist society.

The right of ownership means that changes in the value of an asset are borne by its owner. It also means that the mode of entry into decision making with regard to the use of scarce resources is the prerogative of ownership either directly or through hired managers. The right of ownership then provides for a marriage between decision making and cost bearings. A behavioral implication of this relationship between decision making and cost bearing is that the owner has strong incentives to seek the highest valued use for the asset.

The freedom of contract is a cost-minimizing method for generating information about the set of opportunity choices for scarce resources. The search for voluntarily negotiated exchange reveals relative values that independent but freely interacting individuals attach to the alternative uses of scarce resources.

The government in a capitalist society is expected to enforce the right of ownership, the right of individuals to seek and negotiate voluntary contractual arrangements, and the right to be compensated for damages. In other words, the government in a capitalist society is to enforce rules of the game and to act as the umpire.

> (A stable legal order in capitalism) implies an explicit prejudice in favor of previously existing rights . . . not because change itself is undesirable, but for much more elementary reason that only such a prejudice offers incentives for the emergence of voluntary negotiated settlements among the parties themselves . . . this prejudice [minimizes] resort to the authority of the state.[2]

Although the penalty-reward system associated with the right of ownership provides the decision maker with strong incentives to seek efficient outcomes, the decision maker in government cannot appropriate the full benefit resulting from his action. Nor does he bear the entire cost. No one has a claim on the capitalized value of public assets. Changes in the value of these assets, brought about by allocative decisions, are dissipated throughout the economy. Moreover, pressure groups including all kinds of advocates are concerned only about the benefits that they expect to receive from government expenditures and transfer payments, but these groups are rarely concerned about the costs of these projects. It follows that the penalty-reward system associated with public ownership provides public decision makers with weaker incentives to pursue efficient outcomes. Therein lies the source of objection to governmental controls.

To raise the issue of economic efficiency of capitalism, or of any social system, is to ask whether its prevailing institutions generate behaviors that are consistent with efficient outcomes. Capitalism certainly passes such a test. The freedom of exchange reduces the cost of identifying alternative uses for scarce resources. The right of ownership provides incentives to allocate resources to their highest valued uses. By maintaining and enforcing rules of the game, the government lowers transacting costs.

The vehicle through which the institutions of capitalism promote economic efficiency is profit. Differents in profits among various industries and firms provide quick and reliable information that the allocation of resources requires a correction, that the output-mix is not consistent with the community's demand for various goods, and that some firms are managed inefficiently. Resource owners, driven by their own interests, respond to this information by transferring resources (including managers) to more valuable uses. In the process, differences in profits are competed away via lower prices of goods that were earning above-average profits (due to larger supplies) and higher market valuation of resources used in their production. Changes in technology, incomes, consumers' tastes, and other variables modify the end result of this process of adjustment.

The allocation of resources is then continuously adjusted to conform to changes in the mix of outputs desired by the community.

In a capitalist economy, profit also serves the important function of developing new exchange opportunities (innovations). In effect, innovation is an addition to the community's set of opportunity choices. It denies the community no alternative that was available to it before. The *voluntary* acceptance of a new alternative in the marketplace means that the community considers it superior to previous ones. The innovator is then a true social leader; only those innovators who move the economy in the directions preferred by the community can be successful in the marketplace. A successful innovator has a temporary monopoly position that enables him to earn profits in excess of the opportunity costs. Before too long, the innovator's excess profit will be competed away because others will follow in the wake of a successful innovation. In the end, the community will get the desired amount of that which is new. From the point of view of an individual, a successful innovation is a source of profit. From the point of view of the community, a successful innovation is an engine of progress.

Profit incentives promote economic efficiency at two levels. Those who own or manage scarce resources have incentives to allocate them to the highest valued uses within a given method of production. They also have incentives to seek the lowest cost methods of organization production. Production can be organized both within the market by contractual arrangements (short-term contracts, long-term contracts, contractual allocations of foreseeable risks) and within various types of firms (corporation, partnership, cooperative). Neither method of organizing production is costless.

> Explicitly recognizing that contracting costs are not zero, as they are often assumed to be in economic analysis and explicitly considering the determinants of these costs is the first step in exploring the large variety of contractual and ownership arrangements we observe in the real world.[3]

One may conjecture that contractual arrangements and types of firms that emerge via voluntary negotiation and survive competition from other forms are efficient. In other words, institutions of capitalism generate behaviors that are consistent with efficient outcomes in the market for products as well as the market for organizational forms.

Denigration of Capitalism

The capitalist system promotes the development of individuals, cultivates the strength from confronting risk, and puts a premium on the respect for promises. It encourages self-determination, self-responsibility, and competitivensss. Thus, the capitalist system has a strong moral content. Most moral principles that have survived the test of time promote economic efficiency. The market mechanism attaches costs to the violation of moral principles. A reputation for honest dealing is a source of wealth. Competitive markets weed out crooks, cheaters, and liars. Even though competitive markets do not make people moral, they raise the cost of unethical behavior. As Adam Smith pointed out two hundred years ago, the Dutch, the most commercial of all the nations in Europe at that time (in 1776), were also the most faithful to their word.

Capitalism is then a system that looks out for the common man through efficiency and innovation. It has produced a standard of living that no other system has ever been able to duplicate. Yet the system has never been loved. It is merely tolerated for its superior performance. From within, capitalism has been threatened—and quite successfully—by two sets of forces: a large segment of the academic community and the bureaucrats. The result has been a movement away from limited government and individual freedom and toward pervasive governments as well as collective controls of all activities. As Justice Louis Brandeis pointed out about fifty years ago, when the government's purposes are beneficient, the greatest dangers to liberty lurk in insidious encroachment by zealous well-meaning men without understanding.

Through the government the intellectual community can reshape the community in accordance with its standards of justice and morality. The intellectuals see the government as the best way, indeed the only way, to ensure that economic policies serve the objectives of equality, justice, and happiness for all as they perceive them. The public-policy formation process begins in the minds of intellectuals in the academic community. As Keynes has been alleged to have said, "The ideas of economists and political philosophers, both when they are right and when they are wrong, are more powerful than is commonly understood. . . . Indeed, the world is ruled by little else." Ideas are produced, debated, and formulated in academic communities. Then they are picked up by journalists, editorial writers, media commentators, political activists, and civic leaders. These people translate academic thoughts into public attitudes, beliefs, and calls for action. Congress then approves new programs, and the bureaucracy implements them.

The Federal Register (the carrier of governmental regulations) contained 2,411 pages in 1936, 20,036 in 1970, and over 61,000 in 1979. The cost to the government of administering regulations stood at about $5 billion in 1979. However, the major costs of regulations are those incurred by the private sector. The entire cost of compliance with governmental regulations n 1979 was estimated at about $98 billion. Inflation, low rate of capital formation, steadily rising costs of doing business, and numerous restrictions on individual liberties are consequences of compliance. The cost of these consequences are borne by the community as a whole.

Socialism

In theory, all that socialists did was identify flows of capitalism and set forth two claims: first, that the system is not perfectly efficient and, second, that the distribution of income is unequal. The concept of *economic efficiency* is merely a standard to judge performance. Any real-world economy departs from this ideal standard. The real issue is whether the prevailing set of institutions in a country generates behaviors that are consistent with efficient outcomes. It has already been argued that institutions of capitalism surely pass such a test. The distribution of income in a capitalist society is determined by individual's effort, productivity, inheritance, attitude toward risk, and luck. To simply say that there is great inequality in the distribution of income in capitalism raises the question of with what the distribution is being compared.

The most generally accepted measure of money-income inequality is the Gini coefficient, which may vary from zero (perfect equality) to one (perfect inequality). Lowell Gallaway estimated the Gini coefficients for the United States, Sweden, and the Soviet Union to be 0.32, 0.27, and 0.29, respectively.[4] Gini coefficients indicate that there is no significant difference between the Swedish, the Soviet, and the U.S. income distributions.

In practice, socialist societies have become increasingly bureaucratic. The nature of social life in these countries has moved away from individual freedom and toward pervasive collective controls, and the individual has become a subject of all-embracing collective will. The world contains new and substantial evidence that socialism has failed to duplicate the accomplishments of capitalism.

It is important to make a distinction between socialist states in Eastern Europe and creeping socialism in Western Europe. In the East, capitalist institutions have been abolished. In the West, socialist policies have weakened the institution of capitalism.

Socialism in the East

Socialist regimes in Eastern Europe rest on state ownership of productive assets, administrative planning, and the Communist party. Those three institutions define a Soviet-type social system, determine the character of social life in Eastern Europe, and strengthen the power of the ruling elite in that part of the world. The discussion in this chapter will be limited to the Soviet Union from which the practice of scientific socialism originates.

State ownership of productive assets has two important consequences. First, under a regime of public ownership no individual has a claim on the capitalized value of productive assets. The benefits and costs of allocative decisions are dissipated throughout the economy. Thus, public ownership generates little incentive for decision makers to move scarce resources to their highest valued uses. The second consequence of state ownership is that the mode of entry into decision making is via membership in the ruling elite. These two consequences of state ownership create incentives for decision makers to allocate resources in ways that are expected to perpetuate the power of the ruling group.

The function of administrative planning in the Soviet Union is to replace voluntary contracts with governmental controls over both the content as well as the terms of exchange. Administrative planning then serves the objective of strengthening the Soviet political order. The Communist party determines foreign and domestic objectives in the Soviet Union and monitors their implementation. The best jobs in that country are reserved for members of the party. A member of the party gets promotions easier and faster than other Soviet citizens and finds it less difficult to move up the social and economic ladder. In return, the party leadership requires and gets total and unquestioning obedience from the rank and file. Once the party leadership makes a decision, all party members must support it, and the government bureaucracy must execute it. The cost of questioning the leadership and its decisions is a reduction in one's flow of income and other benefits. The party leadership in the Soviet Union is the Politburo. It is the most powerful body in the country. The Politburo is a self-perpetuating elite which one joins through personal connections and from which one departs by death or in political disgrace.

State ownership of productive assets, administrative planning, and the Communist party are the means through which the party leadership seeks to use scarce resources to strengthen and perpetuate its power. The allocation of resources in the Soviet Union then depends on political requirements of the ruling group.

To use economic policy to serve political ends is not costless. Declining rate of growth, overbureaucratization of the system, failure of Soviet agriculture, poor quality of consumer goods, and inadequate housing are only a few examples of numerous economic problems in the Soviet Union. Those problems were generated by the system itself and should not be attributed to either incompetence or wickedness of Soviet leaders. Three important sources of economic problems in the USSR will now be considered.

First, resources are misallocated because of the difference between the ruling group's demand for fixed assets and the community's valuation of present relative to future consumption. The Soviet government has effective ownership in capital goods. It determines the quantity, quality, and allocation of new capital goods and the use of depreciation allowances. The government can also transfer the existing capital goods from one firm to another. The ruling group derives considerable benefits from investment in fixed assets. The power to determine the pattern of investment, the allocation of new capital goods, and the use of additional output are all sources of utility. The ruling elite has the first claim against increments in national income. High rate of economic growth also serves the ruling group's political objectives at home and abroad.

On the cost side, the ruling group can allocate resources for investment in fixed assets without any appreciable reduction in its own consumption. The cost of investment is borne by the community as a whole. Thus, the rate of capital formation in the USSR should be expected to exceed the rate of investment which would prevail if the group had to bear the cost of investment. Whether the community's rate of voluntary savings can be brought into equality with the planned rate of investment is then an important question.

A Russian has three alternatives for converting his current income into wealth. These are savings deposits, investment in human capital, and investment in jewelry, blue jeans, and rock and roll records. Thus, the rate of income which the community makes available for investment in fixed assets is determined by a single wealth-increasing alternative: savings deposits. Moreover, the rate of interest on savings deposits is fixed by the state and has changed only infrequently. It is then reasonable to assert that the rate of voluntary savings in the Soviet Union is likely to be less than in a private-property capitalist state, other things such as the community's income and time preference being the same.

To satisfy its demand for fixed assets the Soviet government must extract forced savings from the community's current income. A real cost to the ruling group of investment in fixed assets is social tension that arises from the state's interference with the people's valuation of present relative to future consumption. The relationship between the ruling group's gains from the marginal unit of investment and its costs in terms of social dissatisfaction, which can be assumed to increase at no less than a constant rate per additional unit of forced savings, is then a major determinant of the rate of investment in the Soviet Union.

A second source of economic problems in the USSR is the misallocation of resources which is due to the substitution of real resources for money as a resource in the firm's production functions. The determination of the minimum money supply needed for carrying out exchange specified in the plan is important to the ruling group. A deviation from that quantity of money (absolute or relative) could either reduce the extent of planned exchange or support transactions that the ruling group might consider undesirable. A consequence of this view of the role of money is that the Soviet government does not allow firms to keep money balances subject to holding preference. Cash balances create a measure of discretionary freedom for firms and could generate types of exchange that interfere with the plan. Thus, Soviet firms make all payments by transferring budgeted balances from one account to another. Firms are also required to turn all cash receipts promptly to the state bank. Since cash balances are a factor of production, the effect of denying business firms the right to keep cash balances subject to holding preference leads to a substitution of real resources for money as a resource.[5] This substitution means an increase in the cost of negotiating exchange and a reduction in the extent of exchange.

A third source of economic problems is the waste and inefficiencies which are attributed to the high cost of information in the Soviet system of administrative planning. The party leadership sets objectives for the economy. Gosplan then translates those objectives into production targets for business firms, state firms, and collective firms. It sends preliminary targets to various regions, industries, and firms. These preliminary figures are related to the past performance of productive units, new capacities, new priorities, changes in productivity, and so on. Productive units must then send back their comments and suggestions. Of course, they tend to understate what they can do and overstate what they need.

In the Soviet economy, each firm's output depends on the availability of raw materials and intermediary goods produced by other firms. Thus, the economic plan must prescribe not only the outputs of individual firms but also the allocation of inputs. In a market economy, business firms bid for supplies in the market. To allow firms to do the same in a planned economy could easily disturb the plan's objective and frustrate the will of the ruling elite. Thus, Gosplan controls the allocation of about two thousand inputs, and various ministries and lower level bureaucracies allocate another thirty-eight thousand inputs. In total, the Soviet bureaucracy thus controls the allocation and use of about forty thousand inputs.

Firms are told what inputs they will get, in what quantities, from whom, and when to expect deliveries. Supplies often arrive late or never. They also come in wrong quantities. The result is that even a small deviation from the supply plan can easily cause a chain reaction throughout the system. Suppose that a firm that produces screws and bolts fails to deliver them on time to other firms. The rate of output of those firms is immediately affected. In turn, enterprises that depend on that firms' output then become affected, and so on.

The cost of correcting even a minor mistake in the plan is enormous. Suppose that planners detect that the production of screws is lagging behind the planned rate. Clearly, they must increase the allocation of various inputs to the firms producing screws. To do that, they must reduce the allocation of resources to other firms. They must then reduce the planned rate of output of these firms as well as other firms that depend on them, and so on. Every time a mistake in the plan is noticed, the supply and production plans for a number of industries must be revised. When these modifications occur, in effect the plan is constantly revised and brought in line with the business firms' actual performances. Thus, in the course of the year, the plan and the economy's actual performance eventually converge.

For example, the average rate of growth of total industrial output was set at about 8 percent per year in the 1971–75 plan. The actual rate of growth in 1971 and in 1972 fell off to 6.1 percent and 5.4 percent, respectively. Then, the Societ government simply reduced the planned rate of growth to 5.8 percent. In the five-year plan from 1976 to 1980, growth has averaged 4.7 percent compared to the goal of 6.3 percent. Thus, as G.W. Nutter points out, "Through this constant readjustment, current plan and performance converge in the course of time, and it is no wonder that the percentages of plan fulfillment published at the conclusion of each year are generally so high."[6]

It is clear that revisions and adjustments in the plan must result in lower output targets for many firms. The ruling elite must then designate certain sectors of the economy as low-priority areas. Consumer-goods industries have consistently been assigned the task of bearing the cost of miscalculations, inadequacies, and inconsistencies in the plan. In other words, planners need a buffer to absorb mistakes in the plan. In the USSR the consumer fulfills that function.

The Soviet ruling elite lives on the strength of its political power. Soviet bureaucrats and planners live on their service to the ruling elite. Soviet managers prosper if they can fulfill the plan. The Soviet citizen is the lower. The citizen's misfortune lies in the fact that the system of central planning offers no rewards for decisions that take into account his preferences.

Concluding Remarks

Capitalism and socialism are two major social systems in the world today. They are defined by a set of institutions that spring from ideology. Capitalism derives its spiritual force from the basic belief in individual liberty. Socialism is rooted in Marxism. But ideas have consequences. Those consequences are political, social, and economic. They stem from basic institutions of capitalism and socialism; that is, they are traceable to ideology. They also frequently differ from the intent of ideology. The purpose of this chapter is to identify basic institutions of capitalism and socialism and to capture the essence of their effects on economic behavior.

Notes

1. J. Schumpeter, *The Theory of Economic Development* (Cambridge: Harvard University Press, 1959), p. 122.

2. James M. Buchanan, *Freedom in Constitutional Contract* (College Station: Texas A & M Press, 1978), p. 109.

3. B. Klein, R. Crawford, and A. Alchian, "Vertical Integration, Appropriable Rents, and the Competitive Contracting Process," *Journal of Law and Economics* 21(October 1978):325.

4. Lowell Gallaway, "The Folklore of Unemployment and Poverty," in *Governmental Controls and the Free Market,* ed. Svetozar Pejovick (College Station: Texas A & M Press, 1976), p. 49.

5. See Svetozar Pejovick, "Economic References in the Soviet Union," *Modern Age* 16(winter 1972):68–76.

6. G.W. Nutter, *Central Economic Planning* (Washington, D.C.: American Enterprise Institute, 1976), p. 5.

2 The Origins of Capitalism: A Methodological Essay

R. M. Hartwell

The conventional interpretation of the history of Western Europe up to 1914 is that the economic development of the ancient world was interrupted and retarded by the decline and fall of the Roman Empire and by the barbarian migrations that followed. Development was resumed in the eleventh century, and after three centuries of remarkable growth and colonization, it was followed in the mid-fourteenth century by a slowing down associated with the Black Death. Development, expansion, and geographical discoveries resumed again in the fifteenth and sixteenth centuries, culminating in the eighteenth and nineteenth centuries in the industrial revolution. In the period since the medieval revival, each phase of development has been associated with an economic system: *feudalism* from 1000 A.D. to the fourteenth century, *mercantilism* from the fifteenth to the eighteenth centuries, and *laissez-faire* with the industrial revolution. There is, correspondingly, a great deal of literature on feudalism, mercantilism, and industrialization as well as on the transitions between feudalism and mercantilism and between mercantilism and industrialization. However, the literature on the rise of capitalism fits uneasily into this established picture of European development. This voluminous literature traces the history of capitalism from early capitalism, rising some time in the late Middle Ages, to high capitalism, maturing with the industrial revolution, to the late capitalism of the twentieth century. There is hardly an economic historian of England who has not written on the subject—W. Cunningham, G. Unwin, W.J. Ashley, E. Lipson, and R.H. Tawney, for example[1]—and as a European phenomenon, it has attracted the attention of some notable historians, including W. Sombart, M. Weber, H. Pirenne, H. Sée, L. Brentano, A. Fanfani, G. Luzatto, N.S.B. Gras, E.J. Hamilton, and J.U. Nef.[2] With so much attention from so many distinguished minds, there should be no ambiguity about what capitalism is, when it began, what caused it, and how it relates to feudalism, mercantilism, and industrialization. However, such is not the case. There is no agreed definition of capitalism, no agreed dating, no agreed causes, and no agreed theory of the development of capitalism. There is much obscure discussion about the transition from feudalism to capitalism, very little discussion about the transition from capitalism to industrialism, and a great deal on the origin of capitalism.

On what capitalism is, there is remarkable silence or confusion. When Sombart wrote in 1930 that "it cannot be said that a clear cut definition has ever been attempted," this was after a generation of historians had been arguing about capitalism.[3] After another generation of argument, the term still remains elusive; its content varies from historian to historian. In two recent books, *The Transition from Feudalism to Capitalism and Feudalism, Capitalism and Beyond*, capitalism is largely undefined.[4] Is its meaning apparently so well understood as not to require definition? A. Macfarlane's *The Origins of English Individualism* similarly makes no attempt to define capitalism except generally to equate it with individualism and with industrialization.[5] Some authors, however, have been more explicit. Sombart, attempting to redress the gap he found in the literature, defined *capitalism* as "an economic system characterized by the predominance of capital."[6] This definition resembles the vague definitions of other historians of Sombart's generation. Sée argued that "the essential characteristic distinguishing a capitalistic régime from other economic systems is the mobility of capital, which in degree overcomes the obstacles born of time and distance."[7] Cunningham also emphasized capital "as the main instrument in material progress" and saw capitalism as a system characterized by "the intervention of capital."[8] Gras defined capitalism more explicitly as "a system of getting a living through the use of capital,"[9] and Pirenne argued that accumulation of profits was the essential characteristic of capitalism.[10] These are weak definitions, too vague and too general to be of much use in identifying this or that economy as being capitalistic. These definitions are analytically unoperational in that they do not explain the timing and diversity of capitalist systems or organization within those systems. *Predominance, mobility, instrument, intervention, use,* and even *accumulation* are not in turn defined either quantitatively (for example, how much capital is necessary to predominate) or analytically (for example, what is the mechanism whereby capital is made mobile or promotes progress).

If historians have failed to define capitalism carefully, economists with the exception of the socialists generally have rejected *capitalism* as a meaningful concept. As J.A. Schumpeter pointed out, "The term Capitalism was, throughout the nineteenth century, hardly used except by Marxists and writers directly influenced by Marxism."[11] Indeed the use of capitalism as a synonym for laissez-faire was mainly the responsibility of socialist critics who wrote about capitalism with a tone of ethical disapproval. The modern use of capitalism by economists defending it, also, can be seen as the natural defence of a term used pejoratively by socialists.[12] Today it is mainly socialists who try to define capitalism most carefully. Thus G.D.H. Cole wrote that "the term capitalism denotes an economic system in which the greater proportion of economic life, particularly ownership of and investment in production goods, is carried on under private (i.e. nongovernmental) auspices through the process of economic competition and the avowed incentive of profit."[13] This view of capitalism identifies it with the free market, private enterprise, and competition, in contrast with the more desirable conditions of socialism, that is, with state enterprise and planning. Other economists have advanced other criteria: thus capitalism has been identified by the ownership and organization of the means of production (Marx), by capital-intensive means of production (Böhn-Bawerk), by the dominance of "the commercial, financial and industrial bourgeoisie" (Schumpeter), and by "a system that accumulates and makes use of capital as a factor of production" (Dobb). Little wonder that A. Gerschenkron has argued that terms like *capitalism* are not easily understandable or clearly operational and that either simple faith or intellectual recklessness is required to argue that systems referred to as capitalism in different areas are sufficiently alike in all relevant respects.[14]

In so far as there is a consensus, it is a consensus of the left, largely dependent on Karl Marx's analysis and its elaboration by Marxist theorists. Marx formulated an explicit model of the capitalist process, explained how it developed from feudalism into socialism, and provided, at the same time, a theory of history, a critique of capitalism, and an optimism about the future of an inevitable socialism. To Marx the crucial characteristics of capitalism were the mode of production and the social relations of production. Capital and its ownership determined the mode of production; the social relations were determined by the employment relation between the bourgeoisie, who owned the capital, and the proletariat, who had only their labor power to sell. The proletariat were dependent on the bourgeoisie who in their competition for profits were driven to exploit the workers. In the inevitable class conflict that will ensue, socialism will replace capitalism. In the previous transition from feudalism to capitalism there is disagreement among the Marxists about the prime mover, but there is agreement that the relationship between lords and serfs changed significantly with the decline in seigneurial income, the increasing resistance of the peasants to coercive transfers of surplus value, the emergence of a free labor force, and the development of a town bourgeoisie with an increasing accumulation.[15] This scenario, although not generally accepted in this form is so widely propagated by historians of the left that it tends to determine at least the contours of discussion about capitalism and its history. It has been responsible for shifting historical attention away from the realities of feudalism, mercantilism, and industrialization to the search for a phenomenon which allegedly transcends all three yet defies definition, dating, and explanation. This great obfuscation has been a massive emotional and academic disservice to a proper understanding of the past.

Identification and Dating of Capitalism

On the origins of capitalism, in terms of both dating and causation, there is also a great deal of confusion and disagreement. This is not surprising. With different historians seeking different criteria to identify the beginnings of capitalism, and with no agreed formulae to determine what density or quantity of those criteria proves the substantial existence of capitalism, there has been in consequence a variety of identifications and datings. The problem of identification, moreover, has led to theories about the development of capitalism in stages, either in terms of intensity (early, full, and late capitalisms, for example) or in terms of functional characteristics (commercial, industrial, and financial capitalisms, for example).

On dating there are three schools: those who argue for continuity from the capitalism of the ancient world (Brentano and R. Latouche), those who find the origins of capitalism in the medieval world (Pirenne, Sombart, and Fanfani), and those who see capitalism as part of the changes in Europe that followed the Renaissance and Reformation (Weber, Tawney, Hamilton, and Luzzato).[16] Probably most historians agree that whatever capitalism was the decisive changes that brought it into existence had been accomplished by 1600 or even earlier. "By the end of the fifteenth century," Schumpeter argued, "most of the phenomena that we are in the habit of associating with that vague word Capitalism had put in their appearance."[17] There agreement ends. To Brentano, to whom capitalism began in Babylon, modern capitalism owes much to the Crusades and its effects on Mediterranean cities.[18] According to Latouche the Dark Ages from the fourth to the eleventh centuries "brought into being a new Europe . . . facing outward to the Atlantic and the North Sea, and from this new Europe the Western economy took its pattern."[19] H.E. Hallam asserted that medieval agriculture and especially the monasteries inspired, for example, by the Benedictine Rule provided both "the growth of capital and the generation of the right attitude."[20] According to Pirenne, capitalism and commerce on a large scale, which was both its cause and its effect, undoubtedly existed in the twelfth century.[21] Sée stated that, "the town life of the Middle Ages furnished the favourable environment in which the first manifestations of capitalism appeared," although "the most fruitful sources of modern capitalism, without doubt, have been the great maritime discoveries."[22] In the early work of Sombart, capitalism developed from medieval rent, from the landed estates of the aristocracy and from the urban properties of the town patriciate.[23] According to Weber, the Reformation made the decisive break for Europe generally.[24] For Tawney the critical period for capitalism, especially in England, was the two centuries following the Reformation.[25] The Catholic Middle Ages, according to Fanfani, saw the rise of great numbers of early capitalists.[26] H.M. Robertson also found Catholic counterparts for most of the Puritan beliefs which are supposed to demonstrate capitalism's Puritan origins.[27] Hamilton asserted that the profit inflation which followed the import of U.S. bullion into Europe provided the accumulation to launch capitalism.[28] These explanations of the rise of capitalism cannot be divorced, as the authors generally make quite clear, from what they believe capitalism is or from what they believe to be the essential characteristics of capitalism. Thus, the problem of dating and causation remains one of definition, that is, of specifying first what is being identified.

There are three main characteristics which the historians have used both to identify capitalism and also to date its origins: the first centers on the type of economic system, on the ownership of property, and on the method of organizing production; the second on capital accumulation; and the third on the ethos or spirit of acquisitiveness and rationality. The historic presence of the first characteristic is found in the emergence of autonomous producing and trading units outside of the restraints of traditional feudal society. The second is sought in the new or enlarged sources of medieval capital accumulation, either in feudal estates or, more obviously, in towns. The third is discovered in the individualist ethic of the Reformation which freed men from the allegedly anticapitalist commitments of Catholicism. Various historians have tended to use at least two of these characteristics to date the origins of capitalism. Marx (and the Marxists) used the type of economic system and capital accumulation.[29] Sombart used capital accumulation and the capitalist ethic.[30] Brentano used economic organization and the individualist ethic.[31] Sée, a more eclectic historian, used all three.[32] Tawney insisted on the emergence of the acquisitive ethic as the tonic of modern capitalism.[33]

These various explanations and datings of the rise of capitalism are well known and vigorously criticized, and there are others which vary in their attribution of the responsibility for capitalism from the Moslem invasions to the slave trade, or from the rise of a money economy to the rise of the middle classes.[34] They all have in common a dating which, though varied, precedes the industrial revolution, usually by centuries, and an undefined relationship with the industrial revolution. In general historicans agree with M. Dobb that the industrial revolution represented a transition from an early and immature stage of capitalism characterized by increasing accumulation and the dominance of industrial capital.[35] It was an increasing intensity rather than a change in quality. "The phenomena of the sixteenth century," Pirenne wrote of the nineteenth century, "are reproduced, but with tenfold intensity."[36]

When the same historians turn to explain industrialization rather than capitalism, it is significant that their explanations mirror those for capitalism: a changing economic system (freedom of enterprise rather than state control) and organization (the factory instead of cottage industry); a take-off depending on increasing the proportion of the national income accumulated (from 5 to 10 percent); and an individualist ethic strengthened by government action and exemplified by the success of Dissenters and Quakers.[37] Does the fact that what explained capitalism also explains industrialization prove that they are the same phenomenon? When the historians seek the origins of industrialization, their root searching quickly reveals previous industrial revolutions. In the case of England, J.U. Nef discovered one between 1540 and 1640.[38] E.M. Carus-Wilson actually identified an industrial revolution in the thirteenth century.[39] The time schedule for industrialization now becomes as indistinct as that for capitalism. If growth is substituted for industrialization, there is a similar story. A.R. Bridbury argued, for example, that England "between the Settlements and Domesday . . . was transformed by a social revolution" and an agricultural revolution in which "forest and moor were subdued; the heavier soils, an intractable problem to the Romans, grew corn." He forcefully demonstrated that the growth which led ultimately to the industrial revolution began in the later Middle Ages.[40] The twelfth century, according to B.H. Slicher van Bath, was a period of exuberant development in Western and Southern Europe.[41] The central Middle Ages, according to S. Viljoen, was primarily an age of expansion: "Growth and expansion were the hallmarks of the age."[42] Thus capitalism, industrialization, and growth all had their origins in the middle ages, developed healthily in the early modern period, and came to maturity in the eighteenth and nineteenth centuries.

Market Economy

Given the obvious confusion among the historians about capitalism, would it not be better to jettison the whole literature and to begin instead to interpret the history of Western Europe, as conventionally portrayed, from a different perspective? Surely the most useful differentiation of economies, whether of different economies at the same point in time or of the same or different economies over time, is in terms of the economic system, that is, the way in which the decisions about the allocation of resources and about production, consumption, and distribution are made and the method and means by which these decisions are coordinated. The division of economic systems into traditional-collective, command centrally administered, and market-free enterprise is useful analytically and operational historically. Each type describes how economic activities are coordinated in a particular economic system. Each is plainly recognizable with agreed criteria. Each fits particular real-world economies without discomfort and allows also for mixed economies in which the degree of fit varies. Each is free from moral or ethical overtones. All the economies of history, however, even those which approximated an ideal type, have had elements of all three systems within them, although in the major economies of modern Europe the mix has been one of command and market with traditional methods of allocating resources playing a minor role. The mix has varied considerably among economies and over time, but at any time it has not been difficult to designate any particular economy as *command* or *market*.

In the long history of civilization, however, market economies have been important in only two periods: in the ancient world of Greece and Rome and in the modern European economy since the Middle Ages.[43] It is important to emphasize, moreover, that the traditions of economic freedom, so well developed in the ancient world, were never completely lost and that there is a real continuity from fifth century Greece to eighteenth century England. An important historical problem becomes one of determining how periods of comparative economic freedom came into being and why they gave way to periods of economic command. In particular, if the period of ancient free economy survived with fluctuations for a thousand years, why did modern free economies take something like five hundred years to develop within command economies (feudalism and mercantilism), why did they flourish for only a century and a half, and why are they already deteriorating into centrally administered command economies? In this chapter, however, the problem is narrowed down to explaining the successful emergence of a market economy in Europe since the Middle Ages.

If the industrial revolution is seen not as the maturing of capitalism or as the result of a structural change in economic activity but rather as the natural outcome of an increasingly efficient market economy, then the factors over time which made for market efficiency are the important landmarks in the history of industrialization.[44] An efficient market is one in which economic decisions are made competitively with expectations of reward and punishment, profit and loss, according to the successful prediction of market needs and responses. Actions are based on prices, and if there are institutional changes which make prices more accurately reflect demand and supply conditions, then decisions about the allocation of resources can be made more rationally, and the possibility of reward can be made more certain. When finally the market alone is the determinant of allocation decisions, when finally there are no or few extra-market constraints on such decisions, then entrepreneurial and managerial talent can operate productively. It was the gradual freeing of man's entrepreneurial talents from the bonds of custom and command that finally resulted in the remarkable economic growth of the industrial revolution. It was not just economic freedom, however, that heralded this development; it was the gradual establishment of a society in which there was the remarkable release of energy of the eighteenth century.[45] These freedoms came as much from the Reformation and the Renaissance as from the rise of European liberalism in which political democracy and market economy, intimately connected, developed together. The eroding of the moral authority of centrally administered religions as much as the weakening of the political authority of kings and aristocrats, the success of the exuberant individualism of literature and art as much as the possessive individualism of political theory, and the establishment of pluralist societies subject only to the rule of law were all important in widening the range and scope of freedoms.[46] In particular, as Fritz Machlup has pointed out, the growth of freedoms depended crucially on the removal of coercive restraints which the state used to restrict the freedom of individuals.[47] The essential result of all these changes was, in the words of F.H. Knight, "the liberation of both men and things from the prescriptions of authority and tradition."[48] Only then could economic enterprise function with maximum efficiency and the increasingly productive allocation of resources be assured.

The Rise of Commercial Society

In any period before the industrial revolution, continuity and change must be sought not in towns alone but in the countryside where the overwhelming bulk of the population lived and worked. If there was continuity between Rome and the Middle Ages, part of that continuity is to be found, not only in the usual quest for town and trade survivals but in the persistence anywhere of entre-preneurial effort in a world of declining options and declining freedom of action. If there was change in the Middle Ages that increased capital accumulation and aided the development of a capitalist ethic, it is to be found in agriculture, on the manors, and in the monasteries, as much as in the new and growing towns. Hallam claimed that "by the fifth century materialism was hard-grained with the Christian tradition, for it was a part of ancient Rome which Christians could not cast out and Benedict and Gregory alike were unwillingly stained by it."[49] Bene-dictine monasteries with their disciplines or regularity and sustained effort stressed the work ethic as the godly ethic and became model factory estates. Charlemagne's organization of his estates, like Gregory's management of the Papal Estates, was businesslike and accountable. By the early Middle Ages the accumulation of wealth had become, if it had ever ceased to be so, a respectable and desirable occupation for abbots and bishops, no less than for popes and kings. The well-known story of the Cistercians is instructive in this respect for they were largely responsible in the twelfth and thirteenth centuries for trans-forming England into Europe's main source of fine wool. Not all effort went into production and trade. According to Hallam "The good abbot was a building abbot. . . . A great lord with the Abbot of Peterborough was just as ostentatious, as likely to engage in obstentatious consumption, as a sixteenth or nineteenth century capitalist."[50] All monasteries, like manors, produced for a surplus to provide necessities like tools and salt, luxuries like spices and vestments, and homage goods like altar equipment, manuscripts, and sacred emblems. In con-sequence, monastic treatises on farming, like that of Walter of Henley, were severely practical, stressing the need for careful supervision and hard work.[51]

At the same time there were improving and wealth-seeking secular lords. R. Lennard, for example, has shown that there were plenty of improving land-owners in England at the time of Domesday.[52] It was at the demand of such landlords, as well as of abbots, that was such a stimulus to urban developments in both trade and industry. In the growing towns merchants and manufacturers became rich on trade, as is illustrated by the story of St. Godric, who made a fortune before turning to the church.

> For he started by peddling cheap wares through the countryside to the scattered peasantry, and then, little by little, he associated himself with the urban merchants. Thus, in brief, it befell that he who had been used to drag his weary feet through hamlets and open country, commenced, as he grew at once in age and sagacity, to engage in public commerce with his contemporary associates, in forts and castles, in strongholds and cities, and at various shops in the fairs.[53]

This kind of development Pirenne called *commercial capitalism,* and he reckoned that "in the vigour and relative rapidity of its development it may, without exaggeration, he compared with the industrial revolution of the nineteenth century."[54] Behind commerce was industry: woollen and silk manufactures, metallurgical and glass goods, and wine production. Industrial centers were established, for example, Flanders and Brabant for woollens, North Italy for silks, the Meuse Valley for metals, and Bordeaux for wine.[55] Finance evolved with the development of banking, insurance, and the bill of exchange, and with the monasteries becoming veritable credit establishments.[56] The Middle Ages were full of men "seeking their private lucre and singular advantage, without having due care for the prosperity of the community."[57] As Fanfani stated, "Thus in the Catholic Middle Ages, the whole of Western Europe . . . saw the rise of great numbers of early capitalists; saw them at work, intent on evading the constraint of the laws and on procuring privileges from the princes."[58] With the increasing demand for the law to facilitate and protect market transactions, the Law Merchant took form in the Middle Ages, providing the firm basis for the commercial law of later centuries. "The annuity bond, arising out of a personal debt or a war loan, came from medieval law. . . . Similarly the stock certificate . . . Likewise the bill of exchange. . . . The commercial company is also a medieval product. . . . So also the mortgage, with the security of registration, and the deed of trust, as well as the power of attorney, are medieval in origin." Thus Weber summarized legal developments in the evolution of the rational state.[59] The Law Merchant also gave legal recognition to the ownership of movable goods exchanged for a money price, thus giving to such transfers the same status as those protecting the transfer of land. In such ways legal developments matched economic developments, with formal jurisprudence favourable to capitalism.

Summary. The purpose of this historiographical survey was to answer three questions: What is (was) capitalism? When did it first appear? What caused it? The result, obviously, has been unsatisfactory because the historians have been determinedly vague about what they mean by capitalism. Given the lack of specificity of the subject of inquiry, it is not surprising that the consequence has been a confusing literature.

Two other points can be made. First, most historians who have written about capitalism have been hostile to it and have done much to foster an anticapitalist mentality (an opposition to the institutions of modern Western societies which are characterized by varying degrees of market economy and private property). Much of the historical literature on capitalism is polemical, concerned with criticism of contemporary as well as of historical conditions. Second, capitalism preceded theories of capitalism. As even Tawney admitted, "The capitalist spirit is as old as history."[60] It has always existed in man's acquisitiveness and his propensity, in Adam Smith's words, "to truck, barter and exchange one thing for another." Clerics and philosophers on the one hand, and kings and their servants on the other, generated ideas and institutions to inhibit the growth of capitalism or, in a preferable wording, the growth of economic enterprise. However, both followed chronologically the practice of farmers, artisans, and merchants who, at all times in history, have reacted to market opportunities or created them. The very hazards of life—depressions and disasters, wars and party factions—created opportunities with risks which attracted the venturesome and imaginative. Merchants, for example, have seldom been prevented by legal restraints from trading, especially when abroad, and hence have always challenged existing authority and custom, a point made forcefully by both Aristotle and Aquinas. The demand of kings and aristocrats for wars, luxuries, and loans and the need of institutions to transfer wealth (the Church, for example, in the Middle Ages) have always kept enterprise alive. If policies and institutions were often opposed to enterprise, they could not stifle it completely. Indeed, usually opposition led only to greater ingenuity. When rulers learnt that trade was as successful as arms in achieving political ends, policies and institutions were modified. The Crusades, for example, sanctified trade, and allied God and gold in a mutually beneficial relationship. Sombart was correct when he wrote that "the spirit or the economic outlook of capitalism is dominated by three ideas: acquisition, competition and rationality" and that "the objective, institutional order of capitalism is characteristically free. The dominance of economic individualism has its counterpart in the far reaching independence of the individual economic agents."[61]

It is difficult to discover with these criteria what capitalism was and when it had its origins. As regards attitudes, certainly, the spectrum is one of continuity, stretching back to the origins of civilizations. As regards institutions and agents, the spectrum is one of interrupted continuity, with enterprise managing to survive even in the most hostile ideological and institutional context. Capitalism has always been with us. If one accepts the term as a synonym for market economy, it is obvious that degrees of market economy have existed since the beginnings of civilization. The history of capitalism is largely the history of how enterprise over time has coped with institutional and ideological constraints.

Notes

1. W. Cunningham, *The Progress of Capitalism in England* (Cambridge: At the University Press, 1916); G. Unwin, *The Industrial Organization in the Sixteenth and Seventeenth Centuries* (London: Macmillan, 1904); W.J. Ashley, *The Economic Organization of England* (London: Longmans Green, 1914); E. Lipson, *The Economic History of England* (London: Black, 1931); R.H. Tawney, *Religion and the Rise of Capitalism* (London: Murray, 1926).

2. W. Sombart, "Capitalism," in *Encyclopedia of the Social Sciences* (New York: Macmillan, 1930); M. Weber, *The Protestant Ethic and the Spirit of Capitalism* (London: Allen and Unwin, 1930); H. Pirenne, "The Stages in the Social History of Capitalism," *American Historical Review* 19(1913-14);

H. Sée, *Modern Capitalism: Its Origin and Evaluation* (London: Doublas, 1928);
L. Brentano, *Die Anfänge des modernen Kapitalismus* (Munich: K.B. Akademie
der Wissenschaften, 1916); A. Fanfani, *Catholicism, Protestantism and Capitalism* (New York: Sheed and Ward, 1935); G. Luzatto, *Storia Economica L'età
moderna* (Padua, 1934); N.S.B. Gras, *Business and Capitalism* (New York:
Crofts, 1939); E.J. Hamilton, "American Treasure and the Rise of Capitalism,"
Economica 9 (1929); J.U. Nef, *Industry and Government in France and England, 1540-1640* (*Memoirs of the American Philosophical Society* 15, 1940).

3. Sombart, "Capitalism," p. 195.

4. Paul Sweezy et al., *The Transition from Feudalism to Capitalism*
(London: Foundations of History Library, 1976); E. Kamenka and R.S. Neale
(eds.), *Feudalism, Capitalism and Beyond* (London: Arnold, 1975).

5. A. Macfarlane, *The Origins of English Individualism* (Oxford: Blackwell, 1978).

6. Sombart, "Capitalism," p. 196.

7. Sée, *Modern Capitalism*, p. 180.

8. Cunningham, *Progress of Capitalism*, p. 21.

9. Gras, *Business and Capitalism*, p. vii.

10. H. Pirenne, *Economic and Social History of Medieval Europe* (New
York: Harvest, 1937), p. 161-2.

11. J.A. Schumpeter, *History of Economic Analysis* (Oxford University
Press, 1954), p. 552n.

12. For example, M. Friedman's famous polemic, *Capitalism and Freedom*
(University of Chicago Press, 1962).

13. G.D.H. Cole, "Capitalism," in *A Dictionary of the Social Sciences,*
eds. I. Gould and W.L. Kolb, (Glencoe, Ill.: The Free Press of Glencoe, 1964),
p. 70.

14. K. Marx, *Economic and Philosophical Manuscripts of 1844,* ed. D.
Struik (New York: International Publishers, 1964), p. 255; Böhm-Bawerk,
Capital and Interest (South Holland, Ill.: Libertarian Press, 1959) p. 431; J.
Schumpeter, *Capitalism, Socialism and Democracy* (New York: Harper Row,
1942), p. 381; M. Dobb, *Theories of Value and Distribution since Adam Smith*
(Cambridge University Press, 1973); p. 295; A. Gerschenkron, *Economic Backwardness in Historical Perspective* (Cambridge: Harvard University Press, 1962),
p. 94.

15. See R.H. Hilton, "Introduction," in Sweezy et al., *Transition from
Feudalism* for an analysis of the Marxist theories of transition.

16. For these authors, see footnotes 1 and 2. See also, R. Latouche, *The
Birth of Western Economy: Economic Aspects of the Dark Ages* (New York:
Barnes and Noble, 1961).

17. Schumpeter, *History of Economic Analysis,* p. 78.

18. Brentano, *Die Anfänge des modernen Kapitalismus,* part 3.

19. Latouche, *The Birth of Western Economy,* p. 309.

20. H.E. Hallam, "The Medieval Social Picture," in Kamenka and Neale, (eds.), *Feudalism, Capitalism and Beyond*, p. 40.

21. Pirenne, *Economic and Social History*, pp. 160-1.

22. Sée, *Modern Capitalism*, pp. 7, 41.

23. Sombart, "Capitalism," p. 206.

24. M. Weber, *General Economic History* (New York: Collier, 1961), p. 268.

25. Tawney, *Religion and Capitalism*, p. xii.

26. Fanfani, *Catholicism, Protestantism and Capitalism*, p. 170.

27. H.M. Robertson, *Aspects of the Rise of Economic Individualism* (Cambridge: At the University Press, 1933), p. 209.

28. Hamilton, "American Treasure."

29. M. Dobb, "Capitalism," in *Marxism, Communism and West Society: A Comparative Encyclopaedia* (New York: Herder, 1972), p. 386.

30. P. Seligman, "Introduction," in W. Sombart, *Luxury and Capitalism* (Ann Arbor: University of Michigan Press, 1967), p. viii-200.

31. Brentano, *Die Anfänge des modernen Kapitalismus*, part 3.

32. Sée, *Modern Capitalism*, chapters 1, 2, and 3.

33. Tawney, *Religion and Capitalism*, p. 226.

34. R.M. Hartwell, *The Industrial Revolution and Economic Growth* (London: Methuen, 1970), p. 25.

35. M. Dobb, *Studies in the Development of Capitalism* (London: Routledge, 1946), p. 19.

36. Pirenne, "Stages of Capitalism," pp. 500-15.

37. Hartwell, *Industrial Revolution*, pp. 25-6.

38. J.U. Nef, "The Progress of Technology and the Growth of Large-Scale Industry in Great Britain, 1540-1640," *Economic History Review*, 5 (1934).

39. E.M. Carus-Wilson, "An Industrial Revolution in the Thirteenth Century," *Economic History Review* (1941).

40. A.R. Bridbury, *Economic Growth: England in the Later Middle Ages* (London: Allen and Unwin, 1962), p. 115.

41. B.H. Slicher van Bath, *The Agrarian History of Western Europe, A.D. 500-1850* (London: Arnold, 1963), p. 132.

42. S. Viljoen, *Economic Systems in World History* (London: Longmans, 1974), pp. 109, 123.

43. Ibid. for a vigorous exposition of this view.

44. See Hartwell, *Industrial Revolution* for development of this theme.

45. Ibid.

46. The title of a book by C.B. Macpherson, *The Theory of Possessive Individualism* (Oxford University Press, 1964).

47. Fritz Machlup, "Liberalism and the Choice of Freedoms," in *Roads to Freedom*, ed. E. Streissler (London: Routledge, 1969), p. 119.

48. F.H. Knight, "Historical and Theoretical Issues in the Problem of Modern Capitalism," *Journal of Economic and Business History* (1928-9):135.

49. Hallam, "The Medieval Social Picture," p. 49.

50. Ibid., p. 44.

51. S. Baldwin, *Business in the Middle Ages* (New York: Holt, 1937), pp. 9-10.

52. R. Lennard, *Rural England, 1086-1135* (Oxford University Press, 1959).

53. Baldwin, *Business in the Middle Ages,* p. 7.

54. Pirenne, *Economic and Social History,* p. 47.

55. Baldwin, *Business in the Middle Ages,* part 2.

56. Sée, Modern Capitalism, p. 23.

57. W. Cunningham, *Growth of English Industry and Commerce,* 5th ed. (Cambridge: At the University Press, 1915) vol. 291.

58. Fanfani, *Catholicism, Protestantism and Capitalism,* p. 170.

59. Weber, *General Economic History,* p. 252.

60. Tawney, *Religion and Capitalism,* p. 226.

61. Sombart, "Capitalism," pp. 196, 198.

3 Problems of Defining and Explaining Capitalism

Karl-Dieter Opp

The empirical study of capitalism is concerned with three questions. First, when did capitalism emerge and how did it develop? Second, how is the emergence and development of capitalism to be explained, or, put otherwise, what are the causes for the emergence and development of capitalism? Third, what are the effects of capitalism? A major subproblem is: How should the term *capitalism* be defined, or, in other words, what are the phenomena to be explained? This chapter begins with some comments on the concept of capitalism. Then some problems concerning the explanation of capitalism, are explored.

On the Concept of Capitalism

The concept of *capitalism* is used by different authors with different meanings and often in vague ways. Furthermore, it is worth noting that several features usually are used as defining characteristics of capitalism. This may be illustrated by a definition which says that capitalism exists if autonomous producing and trading units, capital accumulation, and an individualistic ethic exist in a society. Here the variables are autonomous producing and trading units with the values yes or no; capital accumulation with the values yes or no; and individualistic ethic with the values yes or no. Thus, the variables are dichotomies.

This procedure of defining capitalism raises several problems. First, which definitional *variables* should be selected? Second, which *values* of the variables being selected should be taken as definitional characteristics? A particular difficulty arises if a quantitative variable is changed into a dichotomous variable. For example, if the variable, degree of capital accumulation in a society, is used as a variable with two values—capital accumulation: yes or no (or high or low)—the problem arises: Where is the breaking point, that is, what degree of capital accumulation is to be classified as high and as low? Some authors decide to choose *ideal types,* that is, extreme values of the defining variables. This choice is burdened with all the problems of ideal type concepts.[1] Thus, the uses of ideal types poses other problems.

The following problems are the most serious and important ones. Assume the two problems mentioned before are solved, that is, the defining variables and their respective values are specified. Now assume one wants to explain the emergence of capitalism. This means that propositions have to be stated specifying conditions under which the set of variables defining the concept of capitalism have exactly the values specified in the definition. Thus, the dependent variable—capitalism—is composed of a set of variables with specific values.

The task of explaining such a complex variable is extremely difficult, and what is more important, it is even not useful. The first problem with such a complex dependent variable is that there may exist causal relationships between the defining variables. For example, in the definition mentioned before, an individualistic ethic (such as the ethic emerging from ascetic Protestantism) presumably has a causal effect on capital accumulation. One disadvantage of a complex dependent variable is that information on the causal relationships between the defining variables is not under consideration. This implies that the whole causal structure of the independent (explaining) variables and the defining variables will not be specified. This is a loss of information which is not desirable in itself. Furthermore, the success of an explanation may be evaluated incorrectly. Assume a defining variable A has a strong causal effect on another defining variable B. Since one treats the complex variable as a whole, one does not know this. Now assume that an independent variable which is not among the defining variables has an effect on B. Since one does not know the effect of A or B, and since A and B are treated as one complex variable, the explained variance of this variable is rather low. Thus the success of the model will be underestimated, at least as far as the explanation of one of the defining variables is concerned.

There is another loss of information in a model with a complex dependent variable. The independent variables may stand in very different relationships to the single defining variables. This will not be discovered since the single defining variables are lumped together. For example, an independent variable may have a high positive effect on the defining variable A and a high negative effect on a defining variable B. If the complex variable is formed by adding the values of the defining variables, one will get an effect of the independent variable which is rather small. The fact that there are strong effects of different signs (positive and negative) is masked because of the use of a complex dependent variable.

These arguments suggest the following strategy: It does not seem useful to define capitalism as a complex variable. It is preferable to use the defining variables of the capitalism concept as separate variables and to try to discover relationships between these variables and find other variables influencing them.

Are there other arguments for this procedure? If the factual behavior is accepted as an argument for methodological rules, one may point to the fact that sociologists and, as far as the author knows, economists and other social scientists usually do not mix separate variables. On the contrary, one tries to find out whether variables have one or more dimensions in order to avoid contaminated variable clusters.

The use of a decomposed capitalism variable has other advantages. The two problems mentioned before can be easily solved. With respect to the selection of the defining variables a social scientist may choose those variables the explanation of which is interesting to social scientists in general. Nobody will presumably object if a social scientist argues in the following way: The aim is to explain, for example, the development of capital accumulation, the number of inventions, the kinds of property rights, and so forth. The term *capitalism* may have been an incentive to select these variables, but since this concept is not used, definitional problems do not arise.

The second problem of choosing the values of the variables which are the defining characteristics of capitalism is eliminated because the variables are used as they are defined. Thus, there is no problem of breaking points in order to construct dichotomies or dubious ideal types.

From all this one may draw the conclusion: Avoid the term *capitalism* altogether. Specify the variables that one wants to explain. If one likes, one may take the term capitalism as a starting point for identifying the variables to be explained.

If one insists on forming a complex variable, then this should be done after the formulation and test of a decomposed causal model. Then one will be able to see the consequences of introducing a complex variable and, thus, which advantages and disadvantages such a construction might have.

Problems of Explaining Capitalism

Two problems related to the explanation of capitalism will now be considered. The first problem concerns the application of theory. The second one refers to the validity of Max Weber's theses on the relationship between Protestantism and capitalism in view of the data which are presented in Alan Macfarlane.[2] Capitalism refers to variables the meaning of which will be specified if it is necessary.

Singular Causes versus General Theory

In the literature about the origins of capitalism two approaches may be discerned. The first consists of an enumeration of singular causal events without any explicit references to an underlying theory. R.M. Hartwell in chapter 2 of this book quotes some of the great many explanations: the crusades, discoveries, the Reformation. Such an approach is faced in particular with the following problem: Why are the respective factors considered to be causal agents and why are other factors not taken into account? An empirical test of the relevance of these factors is extremely difficult. If there are pertinent data, historians themselves are not in agreement about the validity of the data. An example is Macfarlane's book about which one reviewer remarks that it will take some time before one can draw definitive conclusions.[3] If many causes are considered relevant for the emergence and development of capitalism, many cases (in this case societies) are needed for a test in order to reach valid conclusions about the relevance of the factors. So a test of singular-cause assertions seems hardly possible.

Another procedure to explain the emergence and development of capitalism consists of the application of general theories. A prominent example for this approach is the work of D. North and R. Thomas.[4] They explain economic growth from the tenth to the eighteenth centuries in the Western world by applying the economic theory of property rights.

If the theory applied can be considered to be well confirmed, it solves the first problem mentioned previously: A theory states in general conditions which lead to the occurrence of certain effects. So in a particular situation those facts or factors are relevant which fall under the antecedent of a theory. Put otherwise, a general theory is a guide for the selection of those factors which influence the events to be explained. The relevance of factors need not be tested in historical research since a theory is applied from which information about the factors is drawn. Furthermore, if the data are not clear, one may arrive at alternative explanations, that is, one may say: Either the initial conditions of type A or those of type B, and so forth, have caused the facts to be explained. Thus, one arrives at several how-was-it-possible-that explanations.[5] Thus, even if the data are not clear, the explanations are more satisfying than in the single-cause approach.

Hartwell implicitly seems to accept the view that the application of general theories is useful in order to understand the emergence and development of capitalism. According to his thinking, Macfarlane could have established the relationship between individualism and economic change by applying a general theory.

New Facts and an Old Theory: Individualism in England and Weber's Thesis about the Protestant Ethic and the Spirit of Capitalism

Max Weber, who relates certain religious beliefs of ascetic Protestantism to the emergence of capitalism, plays a prominent role in the attempts to explain the emergence of capitalism. This thesis which has been widely discussed—in a bibliography published in 1978, 500 titles are mentioned dealing with this thesis[6] — is challenged anew by Macfarlane. The following will first sketch the argument of Macfarlane and then consider how far Weber's thesis is touched by this argument.

Macfarlane begins with a detailed description of a peasant society which existed before the twentieth century in parts of Asia and Eastern Europe. Among the characteristics of the peasantry were the following: ownership was not individualized but familial; the household was the basic unit of production and consumption; no labor market existed; there was an absence of cash, local exchange, and markets; there was geographic immobility and little division of labor at the local level; production was almost wholly for direct consumption, not for exchange in the market; and marriage occurred at an early age with frequent intravillage marriages. Then Macfarlane analyzes the writings of Macaulay, Marx, and Weber. He argues that these writers assume that England was a peasant society up to the sixteenth century. From about the middle of the fifteenth century changes took place which resulted in a capitalist peasant society and changes from the middle of the eighteenth century on to a modern capitalist society.[7] Most of the rest of the book is addressed to the question of whether England in either the sixteenth or seventeenth century was a peasant society similar to either the classical or west European peasantry.[8] Macfarlane's answer, which he tries to document extensively, is that England was not a peasant society back to the thirteenth century. "It appears to have been an open, mobile, market-oriented and highly centralized nation, different not merely in degree but in kind from the peasantries of Eastern Europe and Asia, though only further research will prove whether this was the case."[9]

Nevertheless it seems worthwhile to ask, If one takes the argument of Macfarlane for granted, which implications can be drawn for theories trying to explain the emergence of capitalism? This question will be narrowed to the thesis of Max Weber. Macfarlane himself is quite clear on this point. Of the general theories of Marx and Weber he states:

> In almost every detail, their views in relation to England in the medieval period appear to be incorrect. . . . it is no longer possible to explain the origins of English individualism in terms of . . . Protestantism . . . If it [capitalism] was present in 1250, it is clear that neither the spread of world trade and colonization, nor Protestantism, can have much to do with its origins.[10]

Do the data Macfarlane presents disconfirm Weber's thesis? If someone asserts that some data falsify Weber's thesis, one should examine, first of all, whether it is really Weber's thesis which is falsified or a thesis which the author thinks to be Weber's thesis. In view of the many misunderstandings of this thesis, it is necessary to sketch what Weber asserted as far as it is relevant in this context. Weber analyzes the logical and psychological consequences of a religious belief system, namely, ascetic Protestantism. This belief system was a causal factor (perhaps one may say a sufficient condition) for a professional ethic (*Berufsethik*). The main features of this ethic are that hard work and the accumulation of capital is rewarding in itself. The accumulated wealth is not consumed or enjoyed but invested. This professional ethic is one factor (and not the only factor) which contributed to the development of capitalism. This very rough sketch of some of the hypotheses of Weber must be sufficient here.

In view of these hypotheses Macfarlane could have argued that capitalism was present already in the thirteenth century. Protestantism developed later in the sixteenth century. Thus, Protestantism could neither be a direct nor an indirect cause of capitalism because Protestantism emerged later than capitalism. This argument sounds convincing, but it is not. The argument is only correct, if the term *capitalism* is used in the same sense by Weber and Macfarlane. This, however, is certainly not the case. Features of modern capitalism in Weber's sense are, for example, investment of capital on a large scale and rational organization of work in enterprisers.[11] Whatever Weber means exactly by capitalism, he refers to quite other phenomena than Macfarlane.[12] Thus, one may conclude that Macfarlane's account, provided one accepts, it, does not at all falsify Weber's thesis. On the contrary, it seems that Macfarlane's account confirms some of Weber's hypotheses or could be used to extend Weber's hypotheses. Weber deals also with conditions for the acceptance of Protestantism and for the emergence of capitalism in the sense described.[13] For the latter he mentions as factors separation of consumption and production units or free labor.[14] These are factors characterizing capitalism or, better, individualism in Macfarlane's sense. So one may speculate that English individualism may be a situation which was conducive to the acceptance of ascetic Protestantism and to the development of capitalism in Weber's sense. Because of limitations of space, these hints must suffice here. The point to be made is that Macfarlane's analysis is not a falsification of Weber's thesis.

Notes

1. See C. Kempel and P. Oppenheim, *Der Typus Gergiff im Lichte den Neumen Logir* (Leiden, 1936), pp. 83-4.

2. Alan Macfarlane, *The Origins of English Individualism* (Oxford: Basil Blackwell, 1978).

3. L. Kurtz, "A. Macfarlane, the Origins of English Individualism," *American Journal of Sociology* 86(1980):403-7.

4. North and R. Thomas, *The Rise of the Western World* (Cambridge: At the University Press, 1973).

5. H. Westmeyer, *Kritik der Psychologischen Unvernunft* Probleme der Psychologie als Wissenschaft (Stuttgart, 1973), pp. 27-30.

6. M. Weber, *Die Protestangische Ethik,* ed. J. Winckelmann, 3rd ed. (Gutersloh, 1978).

7. Macfarlane, *Origins of English Individualism*, p. 34.

8. Ibid., p. 62.

9. Ibid., p. 163.

10. Ibid., pp. 195-198.

11. M. Weber, *Die Protestantinche Ethik,* ed J. Wimckelmann (Munich and Hamburg, 1965), p. 49.

12. R. Bendix, *Max Weber, An Intellectual Portrast* (Garden City, N.J.: Basic Books, 1960), p. 53.

13. M. Weber, *Die Protestantische Ethik* (1965), pp. 32, 52-3.

14. Ibid., pp. 16-7.

4 The Ethics of Capitalism

Peter F. Koslowski

Who would not be bright enough to see much in his surroundings which is, indeed, not as it should be?
　　　　　—Hegel, *Enzyklopädie der philosophischen Wissenchaften* (1830) §6
The world is always only a little short of salvation.
　　　　　—Carl Sternheim, *1913. Aus dem bürgerlichen Heldenleben*

Within the scope of studies on the philosophical and economic foundations of capitalism, the moral inquiry into the ethics and morality of capitalism is certainly most delicate and ambiguous. It must find a path between uncritical apology and presumptuous moralism, between precipitate acceptance of the status quo and abstract imperatives.

Capitalism as an economic order is distinguished by three structural characteristics, namely, private disposal of means of production, market and price mechanisms as means of coordination, and profit and utility maximization. as the basic motivation in economic action. This chapter's thesis is that capitalism is inseparably bound with the history of freedom and subjectivity and constitutes a necessary component of a free society but that a theory of capitalism (as a societal form) which considers the capitalist economic order to be the whole of society falls short of societal reality. All attempts to base society exclusively upon these three structural characteristics fall to the reductionism objection as raised already by neoliberals such as W. Röpke and A. Rüstow.[1] Tendencies of the contemporary positivist economic theory (Becker 1974; Hirshleifer 1978) to make the capitalist economy and its paradigm a universal and conclusive theory of human action and society, indeed, beyond sociobiology to even make it a theory of all life forms, present an interesting theory imperialism of economics but are ultimately economic reductions. These theories cannot ground the conditions for preservation of capitalism; instead they endanger them.

In believing that they can dispose with ethics and with the posing of value questions, contemporary positivist economists overlook that as a society of free individuals, capitalism places enormous moral demands on the individuals and requires a moral attitude that the economy alone cannot produce. Against such attempts it is necessary to recall that economics originated from moral philosophy

A German and slightly enlarged version of this chapter was published in 1982 as a monograph under the title *Ethik des Kapitalismus* edited by the Walter Eucken Institut, Freidburg in Breisgau (Tubingen: J.C.B. Mahr (Paul Siebeck).

and that its father Adam Smith wrote two treatises: *The Wealth of Nations* and *The Theory of Moral Sentiments.* A social philosophy of capitalism must have the same breadth of perspective as Adam Smith. It must guard against committing the economic fallacy of believing that an economically efficient system already makes for a good or moral society and that the economy is the whole of society.

This chapter will first give an overview of the ethical, moral-theological, and metaphysical changes that accompanied the advent of capitalism, that is, a sketch of its *normative genesis.* Then the questions of whether capitalism requires ethics or is at all compatible with ethics and whether capitalism can be justified as a social system will be considered.

What Does Morality of an Economic System Mean?

The question of the morality of capitalism cannot contribute an additional moral aspect to the economic, sociological, and political aspects of the topic of capitalism; rather, it must be understood as the integration and moral evaluation of the totality of arguments. Morality is not one aspect among others, but a way to appreciate the perspectives and arguments of the sciences, to order and evaluate them, and to render them meaningful for human action.[2] The question of the morality of capitalism cannot be, Is capitalism moral? The question must be, Is capitalism justifiable under the conditions of human nature and the scarcity of resources? A principle of the moral theology and natural right of Baroque time stated that moral obligation arises from the nature of the object.[3] The morality of capitalism can be justified only by the nature of the object, that is, the function of the economy and the possibilities it offers for human self-realization. Morality amounts to appropriateness to the matter and cannot consist in the abstract opposition of a moral ought as against economic arguments. As the distinction between descriptive and prescriptive propositions was never fully maintained and an economic natural right of efficiency always prevailed in economics, the question of the morality of capitalism need not fear the naturalistic fallacy because this objection has in some sense itself proved a fallacy. The moral inquiry is not opposed to economic theory but must take up the latter and ask whether all aspects of reality are done justice.

To the understandable objection that this claim to a totality of perspectives in ethics is very extensive, one must answer that people raise the question of the justification of their actions and of the system in this universality and not as an inquiry into single aspects of their existence. In addition, one lives in a totality of social conditions and is determined by them. One would want neither to live in a just society where there is nothing to buy nor in an efficient, rich society that employs its resources for morally reprehensible purposes. In the inquiry into the ethics of capitalism and into the totality of its characteristics, therefore, scientific precision must not be paid for by the renunciation of the entirety of possible aspects. At the same time it is evident that a social order can never be justified once and for all because the number and importance of the viewpoints by which it must be evaluated constantly change with time.

The Development toward Capitalism

The attempt to suitably define *capitalism* causes difficulties since the notion of capitalism is to a great degree laden with negative connotations. An *ism* generally signifies an exaggeration of an otherwise legitimate notion. Consequently, the concept of capitalism, as Röpke justly remarks, "has been made responsible for all suffering, evil and injustice in the world, all of which were beforehand put into the concept of capitalism" (1949), p. 45). Several examples from the 111 different definitions of capitalism that Passow (1927) lists may clarify this. Capitalism is there designated as the spirit of haggling and usury of the jewification of society, mammonism, the bastard of feudal landed property and free market, and the victory of plebeians and parvenus.

The Freeing of Private Property, Profit and Utility Maximization, and Coordination by Markets from Social Restrictions

In contrast to these abuses, occidental capitalism is defined here by three essential structural characteristics which are not limited to capitalism but which bear a particularly distinguished form in it: (1) private property—of means of production as well; (2) profit and utility maximization as economic purposes; and (3) coordination of economic activities by markets and prices.[4] All three structural characteristics can be found in all societies, traditional and modern, but they assume special distinction in capitalist societies. People always have private property at their disposal—at least on the limbs of their bodies. They always pursue the goal of maximum profit besides other goals, and the relative prices for goods and services reflect always, besides other determinants, supply and demand ratios and, thereby, relative scarcity. According to J. Röpke (1970, p. 15), three exchange mechanisms are present in all societies: exchange via markets, exchange by coercion or the threat of coercion, and forms of reciprocal, socially determined exchange (gifts, relations of exchange in families, and so forth). In principle, the types of exchange do not alter, but in modern times and especially in pure capitalism the relative predominance of market, redistribution, and reciprocity relationships shifts toward the market, whereas reciprocal relations that are determined by social and cultural values prevail in traditional societies. Röpke's thesis is confirmed by the research of Shalins who shows that patterns of exchange in traditional societies depend on degrees of kinship to the extent that market principles are applicable only to intertribal trade; the cultural overlapping with and social standardization of economic acts of exchange increases in proportion to the intensity of kinship (1965).

The degree of embeddedness of the market in social and cultural norms and the extent of social and cultural restrictions under which the price system works are higher in traditional than in modern societies. Modern capitalism is distinguished not by its structural characteristics but by the extent of their disembeddedness.[5] This is not only true for the price system but also for profit maximization and property. Maximization of payoff is a fundamental distinction of human rationality, but the emergence of the structure of commercial motivation from religious and cultural contexts is an essential feature of modernity which asserts itself in the Renaissance and mercantilism. It is, therefore, not only capitalistic, but this feature marks the beginning of the economic age. It is not *pleonexia,* that is, nonsatiety, which signifies the advent of capitalism but the moral neutralization of profit maximization as a respectable motive and driving force of the economy.

The process of moral neutralization and social disembeddedness extends to property rights as well. Property is an anthropological constant given by individual corporeality and the individual's disposition over his corporeal instruments. The conceptual pleonasm *private property* which Hegel introduced into philosophical discussion shows a new shade of property rights. Property has become private, its social restrictions reduced, its private rights extended. As G. Fichte realized, the extension of material property rights as free rights of the owner is necessarily accompanied by the abolition of property rights on persons (bondage, serfdom), which means a reembeddedness of property under the moral norm of personal freedom.[6]

The development toward capitalism can be described as the process of autonomization of the economy (Salin 1967).[7] It entails a stronger influence of economic laws on distribution, social structure, the status system, and the stratification of society. It is this emancipation of the economy that evokes anticapitalist critique and procapitalist applause. The question of the morality of capitalism is, therefore, essentially an inquiry into the legitimacy of the moral and cultural neutralization of the three structural characteristics.

The process in which the economy becomes autonomous is a manifestation of the development of the European spirit toward individualization, subjectivization, and rationalization. Thus, it is bound up with the history of freedom in western culture. Individualization means the freeing of man from the constraints of inherited social status and from determination by social and religious norms. This process involves a differentiation between individual and society, which the individual perceives simultaneously as liberation and alienation. It is an indication of the development toward subjectivity. The subject, the I, becomes responsible for its actions and social position. Western individualism finds its basis in the developmental tendency from status to contract and from ascription to achievement.

The origins of western individualism lie, as German idealistic philosophy repeatedly emphasized, in Christianity. The high order of subjectivity is religiously founded in the Christian conception of each man as an image of God, the incarnation of God in the person of one man, the personal character of God, the individual judgment after death, and bodily (individual) salvation. In assertions such as "Christ has freed us for freedom" (Gal. 5:1), the pathos of subjectivity in Christianity comes into force; it measn first of all the moral autonomy of the subject against the law but cannot be restricted to this form of autonomy.[8]

The freedom of the moral subject requires alignment of the economic process with the individual plans of producers and consumers. The indivisibility of freedom demands freedom of commerce and economic value-subjectivism. The contract between consenting partners as the basis for employment and exchange relationships, and the setting of prices according to the individual's subjective evaluation and willingness to pay, reflect the development toward autonomy and subjectivity. Employment relations by assigned status and administered prices correspond to objectified visions of the economy.

The process of individualization and subjectivization is closely allied with that of rationalization, as Max Weber described it.[9] The freeing of individual pursuit of goals and the unrestrained coordination of these goals via the market lead to a form of rationalization which no longer establishes socially obligatory, universal goals and then attempts to socially realize them with minimal costs. This form of rationality attempts with a minimum of expenditure to realize arbitrary goals which are not socially and culturally fixed. Society and economy no longer act value rationally, that is, concerning material values to be reached with the minimum expenditure, which are integrated by way of social values. Rather it acts goal rationally (Max Weber's *zweckrational*), that is, rationally concerning all individual goals, which are integrated into a single market by way of price signals. There is a certain tension between autonomy and value-rationality because the individual regards his own judgment as the standard of value and will find it difficult to accept social values. Within Christian religion the tension between individualization/autonomy and value-rationality first appeared in the Reformation.[10]

The development of occidental culture and society toward capitalism and toward autonomization is laden with a dialectic of freedom, and this, as is often forgotton in economic scientism, is a capacity for both good and evil. The question for social philosophy therefore, is, to what extent the moral and social neutrality of private property, of the maximization of profits, and of the price mechanism can be justified.

The capitalistic understanding of contractual freedom tends to be blind to certain side effects of a moral character. One could characterize these side effects as moral externalities, external effects of the moral qualities of both parties. For example, the seller can take account of the buyer's financial stress in the setting of price.[11] In a restricted market with heterogeneous goods the distribution of producer and consumer rents is not fixed. Moral externalities are possible.

On the other hand, the capitalist paradigm requires the large market with homogeneous goods and the absence of price discrimination, that is, a unitary market price in order to compensate for the moral externalities. According to Adam Smith, whether or not one can obtain meat should not depend on the friendliness or moral quality of the butcher. The old paradigm of justice of contract left the answer to this question to the personal moral judgment: depending on the situation, price discrimination or unitary market price can be morally obligatory.[12]

Side effects are not only a problem for the economy but also a central problem for morality altogether. Freedom of commerce and of contract could only be introduced after it had been proven that external effects, by and large, are internalized so that the pursuit of self-interest (Mandeville's private vices) could bring about positive external effects (public benefits).[13] The question of the permissibility of an action or a contract when there is the possibility of external effects brought about a lengthy moral discussion in the sixteenth and seventeenth centuries, the probabilism dispute. It concerned the question of which authority should be followed when one desires to conclude a contract of questionable (moral) permissibility. May possible side effects be accepted or not? When the party does not conclude a dubious contract, he follows the morality and theologically more certain opinion (opinio tutior). When he concludes it despite his doubts, he follows the less certain opinion, the opinio minus tuta. Whoever concludes a contract for whose permissibility stronger reasons can be given than those opposed follows the probable opinion (opinio probabilior). It is remarkable that probabilism—also named laxism—allows an action when weaker reasons, but nevertheless some reasons, speak for its permissibility.[14] This view first appeared thoroughly stated in the Treaties on the Contracts of Merchants at the beginning of the sixteenth century.[15] The establishment of laxism by the Jesuits in the seventeenth to eighteenth centuries coincided with the rise of capitalism. The weakening of the rigoristic demands of tutiorism concerning the permissibility or nonpermissibility of side effects goes hand in hand with the establishment of freedom of contract. The strict moral conception of just contract corresponds to a stationary, conservative economy, and the subjectivistic conception of morality, that is, the probabilistic morality corresponds to the system of free entrepreneurship. R.H. Coase (1960) has shown that certain discoveries and innovations are economically feasible only when an exclusion or at least a restriction of the liability of producers for side effects is established. It follows that far-reaching technical and social innovations can hardly be introduced if tutiorism prevails, whereas probabilistic criteria may pay too little attention to social costs and externalities. Capitalism, as a system of contractual freedom and technical innovation, historically required the weakening of rigoristic morality and the toleration of external effects. Until now, the problem of externalities has not found a satisfying solution as the example of environmental pollution shows. The moral and theological changes toward probabilism are part of a process of subjectivization and individualization.[16]

The Metaphysics of Capitalism: Katallaxia versus Oikonomia

The question of which economic system is best is not only logically related to the question of whether this is the best of all possible worlds. The answers to both questions always depend on the metaphysics which one advocates and are in a certain sense themselves metaphysical answers.[17] The basic principle of social metaphysics is the correspondence of social and cosmic structure. In western societies this connection is not easily recognized because as pluralistic societies they bring forth a pluralistic metaphysics or what William James called a pluralistic universe.

The concept of economics has its roots in the Greek *oikonomìa*, the household and the administration of the house. Oikonomìa and *oikonomika* originally meant the knowledge of the master of the house (pater familias) as to the direction of the house and his domination of his wife, children, and domestics. The household is, in the words of Walter Eucken, "a simple, centrally directed economy." The old European *oeconomica* is a theory of the whole house as unity of household and business.[18]

To this conception corresponds, then, the conception of the cosmos as the *oikos*. Stoic philosophy saw the cosmos as a thoroughly teleologically ordered whole, as the great household of God, which He directs and protects as the good master. The world is a great oikos consisting of mortals and immortals and directed by a master.[19] The conviction runs from Homer to Thomas Aquinas: "But the things want to be governed not badly, but by *one*."[20]

The same structure appears in economics as in ontology: central government and subordination as principles of order. The world appears to prebourgeois man as the simple, centrally directed economy of God. Wolf Helmhard von Hohberg, one of the major authors of the oeconomica of the seventeenth century, writes in his *Georgica Curiosa* that God "is the charitable, heavenly house master, who never ceases cultivating and ruling over the great world economy."[21] The harmony of divine and human oeconomia is to him self-evident.

The image of the ordered world economy is inseparably bond with a teleological view of human nature in early European metaphysics.[22] The teleological conception of nature and of human action was replaced in a modern period by the mechanical model of Hobbes and Mandeville. The mechanistic model of human nature freed man's commercial strivings because it interpreted desire as boundless and as the power which drove man.[23] It was unable, however, to explain the spontaneous concert of actions.

The justification of the central structural characteristic of capitalism, of the coordination for the common good of the pursuit of individual goals by way of market and price mechanism, requires the assumption that powers of balance are active, that is, a teleological element in a mechanical system. The mediation between mechanism and teleology was accomplished in philosophy by Leibniz's concept of the preestablished harmony, and in economics and social philosophy by the *invisible hand* of Adam Smith. The mechanism model can only explain the mutual effects of utility maximizing individuals on each other, their exertion of force and counterforce, but not the emerging of a spontaneous order, which fulfills the optimality conditions. These are only fulfilled when a conception of preestablished balance is added to the mechanism concept.[24]

Laissez-faire economics found such a concept in the doctrines of Newton on the movement of the stars. Newton's physics, together with the doctrine of the preestablished harmony, were applied to human society.[25] For human society, just as for the starry heaven, there is a preestablished order set up by God, which in its unimpeded workings brings forth the highest standard of happiness and prosperity. Just as the celestial bodies tend toward a harmony of the spheres, the free activities of the economic subjects lead, by means of a process of attraction and repulsion, to a harmony of interests on earth. The theory of laissez-faire and of the market is so optimistically convinced of the wisdom and the power of the creator and of the perfected goodness of creation that, for example, the elder Mirabeau can write: "All direction of the economy by the state either takes place through natural laws, and therefore is superfluous—or it is not successful since it opposes them."[26] Mirabeau calls for the laws of the natural economic order to be posted in all schools, in all city halls, and in all sacristies "as the object of an earthly cult and as a disinfectant against the rampant disease of inhumanity."[27]

Economics corresponds theologically to deism and ontologically to the model of preestablished mechanism. The conceptual difficulties that follow from the relation between human freedom and the natural mechanistic order, on the one hand, and from the relation between God and world in deism, on the other hand, were much neglected during the Enlightenment and were first taken up again in the philosophy of German Idealism. The basic metaphysical principles of deistic theology and social philosophy are identical: absence of domination as opposed to central planning, noninterference as opposed to interventionism, and coordination as opposed to subordination, that is, the standard characteristics of a market society. Just as little as God intervenes in the world, so little should the state intervene in the economy. The paradigm of economics was transformed into the exchange model of economics, into catallactics. *Katallaxìa* replaces oikonomìa.[28] The metaphysical changes lead from a dominating God to a deistic conception of a God who holds himself aloof from the world. The political model changes from hierarchy and subordination to egalitarian democracy and coordination.

Economics itself becomes a part of theodicy. Leibniz used the notion of the preestablished harmony in the *Theodicy* in order to show that this is the best of all possible worlds. The theory of the harmony of interests in Mirabeau also contains a theodicy. In the process of secularization, God's economy of salvation is transformed into an economic history of salvation and a philosophy of history in Saint-Simon and Marx. Irenäus and Tertullian introduced the concept of *oeconomia* into Christian theology as the scene for God's plan for saving mankind. They summarized God's incarnation for the salvation of man in the *economic trinity* and developed the doctrine of God and salvation into a functionally consistent dogma.[29] With deism, a direct intervention of God for the sake of salvation is theologically excluded. Mankind cannot hope for salvation through the divine economy of salvation, but is dependent on the workings of the human economy within the world. After the system of natural freedom and capitalism was unable to fulfill the utopian hopes for overcoming scarcity, the problem of the realization of the best of all possible worlds is transformed into the economic utopia of Karl Marx who had the illusion that the evils of the world could once and for all be overcome by an economic reorganization of the means of production.

The Morals of Capitalism, or Are Morals Superfluous in a Working Market?

The problem of the ethics of capitalism arises within the economic theory in the openness of the system, in the possibility of a trade-off between efficiency and economic freedom.[30] The model of general market equilibrium has no unequivocal, automatic solution but rather remains dependent—because of market failure in the case of externalities, indivisibilities, and so on—upon the metaeconomic determination of the optimal relation between freedom and efficiency. The model for the mechanism of choices leaves open in the last analysis a non-mechanical grade of freedom. How can one balance economically between freedom and efficiency? According to J. Marshak, "the sacrifice of liberty is an organizational cost" (1974, p. 199). However, this does not advance the inquiry as to how this sacrifice of freedom is to be evaluated. This question remains one of a balancing between social values which transcend the purely economic model. One cannot immediately switch to forced allocation at every disturbance of the optimality conditions nor can one, as K.J. Arrow correctly objects, hold non-interference to be the only value (1967, p. 12). The science of choice, welfare economics, is of no help here either as the discussion of the possibility of a social welfare function has shown.[31] A mechanical solution of the overall optimum is not available.

F.H. Knight has critically examined the mechanistic analogy in economics. The general equilibrium model interprets economic behavior in accordance with the analogy of force in which the motive causing an act is understood as *force* (Knight 1969, p. 241). Economics must then be concerned with actions arising from preferences that are not further questioned. The Newtonian concept of force in mechanics has been criticized in physics as metaphysical by Mach and Hertz, but it acquires justification insofar as forces in nature and observable and experimentally reproducible. That is not the case, however, for economic preferences, which are conceived as forces behind the choices of individuals. Preferences have a primarily social character; that is, they are influenced by social status, training, and education, as well as by error. Preferences and choices are not identifiable like force and the effects of force in the natural sciences. Market competition cannot be considered according to the model of force and opposing force which lead to an equilibrium of forces. The mechanism model takes goals, motives, and the preferences of individuals for the given and only accepts considerations as to means. It is a model of adaption in which the individuals' acts of choice are based upon their unquestionably accepted preferences and the force conditions of the market. No value problem arises concerning the selection between goals in accord with certain categories.

Through the acceptance of given, constant goals, the moral problem is reduced to an economic one, and ethics is replaced by economics.[32] Knight sees this "displacement of ethics by a sort of higher economics" in classical economics and in utilitarians like Bentham and J.S. Mill, and it also appears in the case of Spencer (1969, p. 19). Looking at contemporary theoretical discussions one could see sociobiology and bioeconomics as attempts to introduce a universal economics. For utilitarians, who are thoroughgoing hedonists, well-being is the goal of all action. Ethics is then reduced to the optimal allocation of resources for the goal of the greatest pleasure. This goal is empty and formal, and as long as the substance of pleasure is not determined, the maxim of maximization of pleasure means no more than each doing as that person wishes anyway. No help in making selections can be drawn from the concept of the greatest pleasure or utility. On this basis, the individual cannot choose if he does not already know what he wants.

Among the objections to hedonism that have been raised since Plato are that people do not want pleasure or utility but rather seek concrete goods and that they do not desire plain pleasure but distinguish and rank various pleasures. Thus, Plato argues in *Gorgias* that a person interested only in satisfaction should best wish himself an itch, so as to be better able to scratch himself.[33] Max Scheler further criticized hedonism by saying that one cannot attain happiness immediately but rather obtain it "on the back of other activities" (1966, p. 351). One does not play the piano in order to be happy; rather, one can be happy when one knows how to play the piano. One's interest in capitalizing precisely does not obtain the goal when one does not do things for their own sake.

The two approaches just presented, that is, the elimination of ethics from capitalism by means of the mechanism model and the attempt of utilitarianism to make economics into a kind of metaethics, are attempts to avoid the value problem inherent in the selection among goals. Thus, "economics might almost be defined as the art of reducing incommensurables to common terms. It is the art of heroic simplification" (Shackle 1972, p. 10). Both positions amount to the attitude correctly described by K.E. Boulding as "knowing the value of nothing and the price of everything," which means nothing other than that the economy can show the individual the relative prices and the optimal allocation of his resources for certain goals, but cannot relieve him of the choice between goals and values (1967, p. 67).

Formation and Coordination of Preferences: The Coherence of Ethics and Economics

Preferences are not rigidly given and invariable, and the social problem is not merely one of economizing the use of means. Preferences are ethically and socially transmitted; they are formed in individual ethical reflection as well as social interaction. Symbolic interactionism, as was presented by G.H. Mead and W.I. Thomas shows how closely one's view of the world and one's perspective is determined by groups and communities.[34] One sees goods not in themselves but rather in a close weave of perspectives of different reference groups to which one belongs and in the symbolic definitions one gives to the qualities of the goods. According to the Thomas theorem, symbolic definitions of situations that people adopt are real in their consequences. From this point of view, culturally defined needs are as real in their consequences as physiological needs. One can consider needs as constant only in abstraction and in the very short run. De facto, preferences continually change by way of the transformation of institutions and society.

As deliberation upon the correct allocation of resources for given purposes, economics can provide information on the possible extent and opportunity costs of the fulfillment of goals. However, Knight points out that it can "never get beyond the question of whether one end conflicts with another end and if so which is to be sacrificed" (1969, p. 37). In the case of a conflict between competing goals one must abandon the level of scientific economics and use preference rules. Ethically speaking, the question as to which goals an individual in a society sets for himself is more important than the question of how this goal is to be fulfilled.

It is obvious that the ethical and sociological theory of the formation of preferences is logically prior to economics as the theory of the allocation of resources for these preferences. One must ask about the reasonableness of the goals and about the optimal allocation of resources for these goals. Neither of these questions can be reduced to the other. Society is not conceivable as a pure katallaxìa, as the problems of a Paretian social overall optimum show. With a given factor endowment and given preferences, a condition is conceivable in which the complete variability of all quantities and of the anthropological presuppositions for the indifference curves leads to a situation in which no one can improve his position without another being hurt. Can this be interpreted as a real optimum? Let us set aside the problem of the initial distribution of endowments for the moment. It is still apparent that all adaptations in the system are more or less of a strategic character. Preferences were not examined or transformed for rationality or goodness but merely adapted to variations in the environment. The Pareto-optimum cannot, therefore, define social or ethical optimality beyond the economic viewpoint of allocative optimality.

The ethical postulate must still be raised that individuals should vary their effective demand not only according to their own given perferences and accommodate to those of others in the course of exchange in such a way that a Pareto-optimal position is reached, but that they should transform their preferences in an ethical way respecting the preferences of others. They should not only move on the indifference curve but change their system of indifference curves at times. K.E. Boulding claimed that every movement on the indifference curve to a point on the contract curve presupposes a certain indulgence and the absence of jealousy or envy (1964). If one follows this thesis, the Pareto-optimum implies a moral minimum. Yet such a moral minimum in a Pareto system cannot be an optimum in a moral sense.

It is an underestimation of ethical reason and a scientific fallacy to assume that people only adapt their preferences strategically and are unable to transform them with respect to the totality of conditions. The model of the market and the Pareto-optimum acquire an ideological character when they are presented as the last word concerning the theory of action. This is even more so the case with respect to attempts, by way of a recourse to sociobiological and bioeconomic categories, at saving economics as the universal science in view of the objections of anthropology and sociology which point to the cultural and institutional formation of preferences and choices. For example, J. Hirshleifer after having conceded that man being "full of love and hate and sheer cussedness ill fits to the model of economic man," introduces the economic gene in order to save the universality of economics (1978, p. 240). The gene directs the choices of man so that he produces or promotes identical duplicates of his genetic equipment. Clearly, the interest of the social biologist is to eliminate acts of choice in a strict sense. No longer the man but rather the economic gene is the doer behind the deed who attempts to strategically secure identical copies of itself. Here the choice between competing values is eliminated; there can no longer be any choice between conflicting goals. The unitary goal of nature and society is simply given and all actions are merely strategically resisted to it. Apart from the animistic element in this theory and the conflicting empirical fact that with sinking birthrates especially wealthy societies do not contribute to the maximization of identical gene copies, although they could do so best, the theory of sociobiology presents the most reductionist interpretation of the value problem. However, sociobiology, contrary to its critics' assertions, is not a theory of capitalism since capitalism does not restrict itself to purposes of genetic reproduction but rather admits all individual purposes—biological, economic, and cultural.

The value problem in capitalism arises because it is not centrally predetermined, and individual evaluation of goals, that is, freedom, is held to be a value. Freedom is both a fact—as nonintervention—and a value category.[35] It can be seen as an instrument for reaching other goods as well as being a value in itself. The understanding of freedom as pure noninterference with market forces eventually leads to a pure mechanism in which everything that occurs without political intervention appears good. This understanding of freedom can be seen in Spencerism and social Darwinism. In western societies, freedom, understood as the ability to act according to self-chosen goals, is seen as an intrinsic value which has pushed other values, such as stability, calculability, and personal continuity into the background. The concept of freedom is bound up with the dialectic of freedom and self-responsibility, without which a free capitalistic order is unthinkable. This burden of freedom brings about the fact that a free economy cannot be, as it were, derived from efficiency criteria, but rather presupposes a moral will to freedom. Freedom and property must be willed.[36]

Capitalism as the system of contractural labor relations and free entrepreneurship excludes the finalization of the economic process according to centrally set goals, that is, the household model of the economy. It does not eliminate the problem of value; it rather puts the burden on the individual. Economic individualism therefore, is, necessarily tied to ethical individualism. The problem of economic individualism is the following: What must I do in order to optimally reach my goal under the given constraints, and under the condition that others pursue their goals? The ethical problem is, What should I want? What are reasonable preferences? The answer of ethical individualism is outlined in the *Critique of Practical Reason* by Kant, who must be considered the founder of the philosophical ethics that correspond to a market economy: "So act that the maxime of your will could at any time serve as a principle of universal legislation." This ethics corresponds to the structural characteristics of capitalism: individualization, autonomization, and universalization.[37] It is, as in the case of a catallactic economy, not finalized but mediates between formal and individual goals. It attempts to provide a criterion, according to which it can be determined whether or not one's individual goals are compatible with those of all others. If the individual goals pass this test, on the next level the question arises: How can these goals coexist with each other in the reality of the economic sphere?

The same objection to Kantian ethics has been made as was raised against the Pareto criterion. It is not capable of providing an answer to the basic problem of practical philosophy: What should we do? The categorical imperative is more a criterion of negative rejection than a procedure for the selection of goals. One cannot live without values as criteria for deliberation between alternative courses of action. In this case, the bounds of rule-directed, methodical thought appear. The good can neither be determined solely as universalization nor expressed as a single category of value. In the selection of alternative forms of action one remains tied to the totality of the situation and of value categories, and one must treat the situation for action as a whole. It is one of the basic insights of philosophy that the good cannot be expressed in a single principle or value, but rather it must be determined as the totality of aspects of a situation and the nature of the matter. The idea of the good, according to Plato, cannot be presented as one single principle but rather as *truth*, that is, as the emergence of that which a thing or person can be if it realizes the possibilities inherent to its nature (*aletheia*) as *beauty* and *measure*.[38] Such a notion of the good certainly invokes methodological objections from a scientific point of view to which Knight replies:

> This is of course intellectually unsatisfactory. The scientific mind can rest only in one or two extreme positions, that there are absolute values, or that every individual desire is an absolute and one as "good" as another. But neither of these is true; we must learn to think in terms of "value-standards" which have validity of a more subtle kind (1969, p. 40).[39]

The difficulty of making operationable such an ethic of the balancing of the totality of aspects puts quite a burden on the moral fantasy of the individual, but the ability to deceive oneself as to possible relevant aspects of an issue to be decided is one of the characteristics of the immoral. The obligation to consider the totality of perspectives can compensate for the lack of operationality by the absence of a dogmatism of rules and a better consideration of possible side effects.

The Need for a Business Ethics

Dogmatism of rules can be best illustrated by W.J. Baumol's dictum that the market cannot sustain a noneconomic ethics and that the automatism of competition renders an ethics of business superfluous. Under the conditions of perfect competition, voluntary moral acts of a single entrepreneur—such as ecological measurements, training for handicapped, and so forth—are not desirable for Baumol since the moral entrepreneur will be thrown out of the market within a short time. According to Baumol, "The merciless market is the consumer's best friend" (Phelps 1975, p. 46). Voluntary supererogation only hurts the single businessman. Baumol asserts that social measures should be enforced by government on all firms.

> Firms should not be all-purpose institutions, but make money for their stockholders. The notion that firms should by themselves pursue the objectives of society is, in fact, a rather frightening proposition . . . Corporate management holds in its hands enormous financial resources. I do not want management to use the capital I have entrusted to it to impose its notions of international morality on the world (Phelps 1975, pp. 46–47).

Baumol's dislike of moralism in corporate management derives from an unjustified optimism about the functioning of the mechanism of competition. Only if all firms produced on the break-even point and there were no producer rents, would every producer who fulfills supererogative actions be driven out of the market place. This case is very unlikely. Producers who produce with costs below the break-even point can afford moral voluntarism very well. In oligopolistic markets, managers can trade off slack for profitability (Williamson 1977, p. 188). They can choose between an easy life for the management and profit maximization. Therefore, they can choose between slack and moral actions as well.[40] Baumol's position shows the fallacy of the mechanistic model. In reality, the alternatives for actions allowed by the economy are much more complex than the classical minimal cost-profit maximization model suggests. Economic practice always takes place in a social totality in which the consideration of additional aspects of economic action which transcend the model of economic man is not only moral but can be profitable as well. Moral actions can have spillovers in profits.

There is a certain irrational passion for dispassionate rationality in the economic theory of capitalism which bans any kind of moral motivation or thinking in terms of values from social science. It endangers the conditions of conservation of economic rationality.[41] As an example take A.A. Alchian and H. Demsetz's theory of the entrepreneur as the monitor of firm members' shirking: "Every team member would prefer a team in which no one, not even himself, shirked. Then the true marginal costs and values could be equated to achieve more preferred positions. . . . Obviously the team is better with team spirit and loyalty, because of reduced shirking—not because of some other feature inherent in loyalty or spirit as such" (1977, p. 101). Here the economist's belief in what Dennis Robertson calls the "need for economizing on love" goes too far. Critique of ideology adopts an ideological character itself when it denies the intrinsic value of moral action or constructs an opposition between morality and advantage, which ethical theory always has doubted. The ethics and particularly the natural right tradition has always—with the exception of Kant—claimed that there is an accordance of morality and enlightened self-interest. This accordance has recently even been confirmed by economic theory.

Sauermann and his colleagues have proven that trust reduces bargaining costs.[42] J.M. Buchanan shows that ethics substitute for direct control in large groups where this control would be costly and are designed to solve the large number dilemma (1965, p. 8; 1978, pp. 364-8). General belief in ethical norms can solve the isolation paradox that each person would do (the) good if he knew that the others would do so too, but will not do it if he might be the only moral individaul in the group (Sen 1967, p. 112; 1973, p. 119). It changes the prisoner's dilemma into an assurance game. Moral codes can be interpreted as reactions of society to the compensation of market failures. Moral codes can lower transaction costs and thus leave everyone better off (Arrow 1971, p. 22). E.C. Banfield shows that the absence of trust and social integration and the predominance of nonenlightened self-interest is an obstacle to economic growth

(1958, p. 89). Transaction costs cause the shift of transactions from the market into firms, which form internal markets for labor and capital (m-form structure, holding corporation). These internal markets are more integrated than the general market by corporation-specific behavioral codes (corporate ethics, corporate philosophy). They increase the conformity between firm members' actual and expected behaviour and reduce transaction costs (Williamson 1977 and 1981). Even the mechanistic model of general market equilibrium shows the need for an ethics of capitalism and for evaluating and choosing between goals. It shows the necessity of bringing mind back in and reembedding business into ethical and social norms.

The Morality of Capitalism and the Limits of Its Justification

According to R.A. Posner, "in a world of scarce resources, waste should be regarded as immoral" (1977, p. 23). Posner's statement could be read as a tautology with which everybody agrees: Waste is a pejorative notion, and no one would call waste moral. In the context of positivist economics, however, this sentence stands for a tendency to regard the allocation problem as the only ethical-economic problem since ethical judgments concerning goals are considered unscientific. In this perspective, capitalism would be the most moral system since it undoubtedly solves the allocation problem with the least waste as compared to other systems.

Nevertheless, one cannot stop asking questions at the point of the allocation problem as was demonstrated in the discussion of individual ethics. For a justification of capitalism, the distribution resulting from an optimal allocation of resources must be investigated, as well as the question of whether capitalism selects or filters out certain goals in the market process. The apologists of capitalism have continually attempted to evade both questions by representing allocation and distribution as simultaneous processes (marginal productivity theory) and disputing the selectivity of the market in pointing out that everyone, according to his willingness to pay, could realize all of his goals in the market. Both arguments are correct but not the whole truth. The arguments are connected. It is correct that allocation and distribution must go together, for otherwise there would be no incentives for an optimal allocation. Moreover, the positive contribution of a productive factor to the total product is one criterion of just distribution, and the consumer's willingness to pay for a given good is one standard for the intensity of preference. Goods should go to those who desire them most intensively, and because this can hardly be determined other than through willingness to pay, therefore, to those who are prepared to pay the most.

A competitive market does lead to the employment of every productive factor when it can bring forth the greatest product, measured in prices, and leads to a distribution which reflects productivity and relative scarcity. This argument from efficiency is not a sufficient ground for the morality of the distribution which results from the remuneration according to a factor's marginal productivity. Even if the problem of economic computation could be solved, the problem of moral computation would remain. All property rights on resources, whether labor (human capital) or capital in general arise from three sources: effort, inheritance, and luck (Knight 1969, p. 56). Of these, only the first source can doubtlessly be called just, the second is merely legal, and the third incommensurable with justice. Thus, the distribution which arises from these three factors cannot be considered moral in an emphatic sense, but only be considered not immoral. Scarcity rents stand for the accidental characteristics of the distribution in the market process. Certain factors are scarce, given to their owners only by an accident of nature, yet are in demand. Other factors are just as scarce but not demanded. Is this sufficient reason to justify the enormous difference in distribution between both of the owners? Hayek's (1977) and R. Nozick's (1974) approach that the distribution must be accepted as the result of a game that proceeds according to impartial rules and cannot be manipulated leaves the moralists unsatisfied and cannot even please the players. After a certain point in time each game requires a new dealing of the cards, a re-creation of the same initial conditions. For the game of life, which we can only play once, this must be even more true. A continual, periodic equalization of the initial positions is for reasons of efficiency not possible and criteria for such a distribution are lacking. Natural differences cannot be redistributed. But one cannot, as Nozik has suggested, disqualify every conception of end state in a theory of justice with reference to the rules of the game. That would be the capitalistic reversal of the dictum, let justice be done, though the world period (fiat justitia ut pereat mundus), into the principle that the rules of the game must be obeyed, even when the chances in the game are very uneven, and even when the end results can be predicted and are trivial.

A purely deontological entitlement theory of justice is as abstract as a consequentionalist theory of end-state justice that continually shapes society in accord with its image of end-state justice. Hegel's remark in *Philosophy of Right* on ethical principles applies to both: "The principle of scorning the consequences of action, and the other, of judging actions by their consequences and making them the standard of what is right and good are both abstract understanding." The unquestioned acceptance of the primary distribution which results from the market in capitalism without giving consideration to the final social effects of the effects of the economic process is no more moral than an arbitrary redistribution that is continually reshaping society and economy according to a prefabricated image of social justice.

Since distribution and selectivity of the market are correlated, both problems reinforce their respective advantages and disadvantages. An economy solely grounded on marginal productivity and effective demand results in an unequal distribution and means that the wealthy succeed better in enforcing their goals in the market. Nevertheless, this inequality can be compensated for by the fact that the consumer needs of the lower income classes become more homogeneous and therefore, can, be satisfied at lower relative prices if in the production of mass goods economies of scale appear. The position of the consumer in the market who has a low income and particular preferences becomes problematic. The same is true for the position of those producers who have a valuable good to offer for which there is no effective mass or elite demand. The extremely subjectivist theory of value which would hold that under these conditions the good in question is not really a valuable good ignores the reality of the market, which is always determined by the whims and ignorance of the public.[43]

Industrial mass production and the buying power of majority taste cause an egalitarian tendency in capitalism that is often overlooked—despite all attention to developments in income distribution. It causes a tendency for the assimilation of life-styles behind the unequal income distribution. This tendency stands in contrast to the fact that one of the main and correct arguments for capitalism is that it makes individual life-styles and ways of life possible to an extent no other economic system did or does.[44] Consumer sovereignty puts the Janus-headed character of capitalism between egalitarianism and luxury and between freedom from domination and monopoly power. The fixation of prices according to demand and supply only removes all feudal privileges and causes a sociological equalization. On the other hand, it sets preferences and demand free of all social restraints or aesthetic criteria and allows parvenu luxury just as well as personal austerity. The market removes social barriers, on the one hand, and creates economic inequality, on the other hand, by the enormous accumulation of wealth as rewards for successful innovations or as quasi rents. The tolerance of capitalistic societies toward the accumulation of wealth and the lacking embeddedness of wealth in ethical or social norms is certainly one of the criterical points of capitalism. It makes the need felt for a new awareness of legitimacy and social obligation among the economic elite.

With respect to the problem of power, Buchanan (1954a and 1954b) has referred to the structural relationship between the market and voting, that is, between the dollar vote and the equal right to vote at the ballot. Markets and democracy both require that decisions be made on the basis of individual preferences. As the Condorcet-Arrow paradox has shown, the market or the dollar vote is much more successful than voting in doing so. The market can register the intensity of preferences which are expressed by the individual's willingness to pay, and it forces the individual who must cast the dollar votes to a greater expression of his preferences and to greater responsibility in his decisions. The market increases by its continuity and nonrestrictedness of decision alternatives the individual's chances to participate in decision making.

Nonetheless, there remains a feeling of moral dissatisfaction with the market mechanism that cannot be explained merely by the inequality of the initial distribution and, therefore, by the greater choice possibilities of inherited wealth.

That the market be moral and the point it chooses on the production possibility frontier be reasonable would require that the effective demand, that is, the preferences of consumers were moral and their knowledge perfect. No one could assert that the choice decisions in the market are on the whole ideal or reasonable. Too much nonsense, bad taste, and superfluous luxury wins out over necessary, meaningful, and beautiful goods. In addition, not only are given preferences coordinated and streams of factors directed through demanded production of goods, but new needs are created through the market as well. As Knight points out, "The economic system forms, transforms, even creates wants. An examination of the ethics of the economic system must consider the question of the kind of wants which it tends to generate or nourish as well as its treatment of wants as they exist at any given time" (1969, p. 46). The moral guilt for many nonsensical needs is not to be borne alone by firms, which want to introduce new goods, but rather by the drive to imitation and the prestige needs of consumers.

It is thus rather remarkable that the proponents of economic democracy criticize the capitalistic system. For if consumers are incapable of asserting their sovereignty as consumers who are opposed to commercial advertising, they cannot begin with the presupposition that the choice makers in a democracy would be able to maintain their choice sovereignty with respect to political advertising in a plebicitary democracy. Both kind of consumer sovereignty which is detached from all religious, aesthetic, and moral norms, and a market system which is entirely oriented toward subjective needs are just as much a cause for fear as a plebicitary democracy without constitutional and legal norms. The market system has always brought forth the criticism from religious quarters which expressed the opinion that the market system gave too much room to human irrationality and overly trusted the ability of human reason.[45] In contrast to the interpretation of Edward R. Norman (1979, p. 10) and J.V. Schall (1979), according to which capitalism is conceived upon a pessimistic anthropology based on original sin, the conception of a subjectivist and domination-free market represents the result of an optimistic, enlightened anthropology, as was shown previously in the case of Mirabeau. One cannot dismiss the religious critique as paternalism. As Max Sheler asserted, "We all believe either in Gods or idols" (1966). When the religious formation of preferences is abandoned, other forces for molding preferences, other Gods and idols appear.

A pure catallaxy is an ideal of coordination but not a meaningful social program because one does not come into the world as a freely decision-making being and utility-maximizing economic man, but is rather subjected to the influence of the environment and of the social reference groups to which one belongs. One needs the institutions and the action-directing norms just as much as, occasionally, paternalistic direction. The theory of market failure and of free-rider behavior with respect to public goods shows this. A society built on revealed preferences only would not be a nice place in which to live. When under certain conditions the methodological individualism of the market leads to fallacies of composition, that is, the fallacy that what is good for the individual is also good for the whole, then this should be true of the voting process as well. Under these conditions, nothing is to be gained by the transfer from the market to a plebicitary democracy. It is much more to be feared that the needs which are not fulfilled in the market (public goods, cultural goods, the environment) would not be properly considered in an ideal democratic process as well. A good portion of the critique of capitalism is equally a critique of democracy and a critique of the inability of individuals to make reasonable use of their consumer sovereignty.

The strengths of capitalism, that it can admit of many goals and of many values insofar as they can be borne by the market and that it abandons the attempt to finalize social and economic processes, are weaknesses in the eyes of those who hold that the market does not properly deal with certain values. Criteria is not available which would tell in which succession or in which intensity values and goals should be realized by the economy. Because freedom in the first place means the ability to set goals for oneself (Kant), one must concede to the economic actors the freedom to set goals for themselves even if one knows better in which order these goals are to be realized.

However, objections must be raised against the *value agnosticism* of capitalism—to the effect that one does not have available any criteria at all. Freedom cannot be the only value which a society can further. One cannot hold an allocation mechanism for a morality which, as Malthus writes, "denies a man a right to subsistence when his labor will not fairly purchase it." The justification for the nonfinalization of the economy in wealthy countries can only go as far as the basic needs have been secured.

That capitalism, despite its successes, has such a bad reputation is to be regarded as a result of the not understood problem of the nonfinalization of the economy. Almost every group considers its own goals to be insufficiently provided for by the market system because the goals of the market system cannot be fixed by it. Farmers see their market results as being insufficient, as do artists and philosophers. That the intellectuals are especially active in the critique of capitalism is caused, as Norman (1979) has clearly shown for the English tradition of capitalism critique, by the fact that they view their goals as not being sufficiently encouraged because of the lack of mass demand. This is certainly the case for representatives of the social sciences. Capitalism with its trust in spontaneous, unplanned order offers them little opportunity for the implementation of their knowledge. In this respect capitalism contrasts with planned economies, which by definition must make the social planner the director of the economic process.

It can not be denied, on the other hand, that capitalism also favors a certain group as far as the distributional results are concerned, namely, the group that fulfills best the conditions and expectations on which the economic system is based: the group of successful entrepreneurs. Nevertheless, it severely punishes the same group if it does not fulfill the system's expectations: the unsuccessful entrepreneur. Every conceivable system always favors the type that corresponds best to its definition. Planned economies favor the planner, theocratic societies the priest, and belligerent societies the military. Capitalism has here the advantage that the fulfillment of system and role expectations and, therefore, social remuneration are efficiently connected with the interests and needs of the population, that is, with consumer demand. The consumers' possibility for exit in a competitive market and the control of profits by competition between producers assure to a certain extent that economic success and remuneration is bound to socially desirable and useful performance (Hirschman 1970).

Against the critique of interest groups upon the allocation and distribution effects of a nonfinalized capitalistic economy, one must recall one of the oldest views of justice in the European tradition, the idea of balance and measure.[46] The idea of a balanced totality of goals and ends must be aimed at the critics of capitalism as well as at the absolutizing of the allocation mechanism of the market. The theory of market failure as well as that of government failure indicates that a balance must be found between society and state, market and voting.[47] Both the market mechanism and the state show their failures. The morality of capitalism cannot consist, as Knight has shown, in introducing abstract economics as absolute ethics, that is, in reducing all question of social and ethical values to the question of the optimal allocation of resources for satisfying given individual preferences (1966). The moral justification of capitalism consists rather in mediating many goals and their pursuit by individuals in such a way as to preserve moral and economic freedom without a war of all against all. That which the individual and society takes to be preferred can only be reached by the market through a compromise between what the individual takes to be important and that what all others take to be important. A compromise is all that can be reached when individual pursuit of goals is allowed. The competition on the market is a kind of institutionalized civil war. "In case it goes out, we are threatened with a kind of pensionier's existence at the expense of the state, even though the competition of states among each other persists. Terror fills this gap," E. Jünger asserts (1952, p. 37). The terror of the social determination of goals by one group is the alternative to competition in advanced societies because, as historical experience shows, only through terror can a society which has experienced freedom be sworn to a particular goal. This is shown by the experience of east European planned economies.

Some Social-Philosophical Conclusions

In historical knowledge, a purely capitalistic society, built exclusively upon private property, maximization of profit, and coordination by way of a market and price system, has not yet been a reality. As a societal model, capitalism bears utopian, contrafactual feature; it is itself a social utopia. Its utopian character always becomes evident when its defenders seek to immunize opponents' objections with the incompleteness argument, that is, by pointing out that it has never been realized in its pure form and that its shortcomings can always be traced to exogenous influences. Such a procedure is not justifiable from an ethical standpoint. A social theory must adjust itself to reality and take its historical locus and historical conditions of realization into account. A theory that presents a superior model but can never be realized due to exogenous influences or nonproducible preconditions is a bad utopia and remains in the "precociousness of the ought" (Hegel).

As a theory of society, capitalism cannot suffice because it is essentially an economic theory of production, exchange, and coordination. As an economic theory, it must neglect essential aspects of social action and political integration. In this chapter, this omission of problem in capitalist theory has been exhibited above all in the assumption of given preferences in economic theory but also in the limits to the principle of coordination market. In both cases, the cause is to be found in an exaggerated methodical individualism and subjectivism, which assumes one can neglect the social mediation of one's preferences and the obligation to have reasonable preferences for the sake of individual freedom of choice. By making freedom and efficiency the sole guiding values in its ideal of coordination, the theory of capitalism evades the problem of comparing goods and gains its most impressive comprehensiveness in general equilibrium analysis. The problem of weighing goods against one another cannot be avoided. This was already seen with the necessity of weighing efficiency against freedom in the selection of allocation mechanisms.

The necessity of comparing goods also turns up in the preference formation of the individual, which cannot be regarded as a black box from which factual preferences pass into actions of choice. The mechanism model of actions of choice as effects of inexaminable forces, the preferences, successfully avoids illuminating the black box *preference formation.* Precisely the preference formation gains significance when with increasing social wealth and material satiation the production problem becomes less urgent.[48]

This satiation also demonstrates the limitation of a concept of freedom that understands freedom merely as freedom of choice between the greatest number of possibilities. A growing supply of goods shows that one does not feel freer when he has greater possibilities of choice among goods, but rather than the marginal utility of freedom of choice also is decreasing. Too many possibilities is just as unpleasant as too few alternatives, not merely due to overburdening of decision and problems of cognitive dissonance after consumption decisions but because this concept of freedom systematically hits only one part of what human freedom is. Philosophical criticism caricatured the understanding of freedom as freedom of choice in the High Middle Ages with Buridan's ass, which starves because it cannot decide between two hay stacks of equal size, and since Kant as the freedom of a turnspit. Moreover, in the mechanism model of general equilibrium theory there can be no real freedom. The agent is determined by his preferences and mechanically adapts himself by his consumption and production decisions to the prevalent market conditions.

Against this conception of economic freedom it must be stressed that freedom primarily means the ability to act according to self-chosen purposes, and that the choice of these purposes or the formation of preferences must be understood as a self-choice, that is, a decision about one's own being and personality.[49] It follows that the concentration of economic theory upon consumption and consumption decision as the purpose of human and, in particular, economic action is one-sided because the personality forms itself essentially in its action not in its consumption. This means that an examination of the extent to which the constitution of an economy admits free action and self-realization cannot be based merely on freedom of consumption. The indubitable superiority of the market as a means of coordination manifests itself here in that it permits individual pursuit of goals and self-responsible action to a greater extent than all other forms of coordination, in that the market permits not only freedom of consumption, but also freedom of action.

It also turns out that maximization of profit and benefits as an economic motive, and free disposition of private property assume a characteristic abstractness when they lay claim to unlimited social validity. The maximization of profit and benefits can only be admitted as motives under constraints; otherwise they reduce the wealth of human motivation to abstractions of rationality and ignore the social embeddedness of the purusit of goals. The same is true of rights of disposition over private property. The coordination of individual actions in capitalism must occur within a social framework which the conditions of this coordination—private property, maximization of profit and utility, and the market system—do not adequately determine, but rather presuppose.[50]

The limits of capitalism as a social theory are that the coordination does not comprise the whole, that the medium is not the message, and that the form of economic action does not fully comprise the substance of one's social action. As a social theory, capitalism is *materially underdetermined* and incomplete. It must be complemented by a comprehensive social-philosophical theory concerning the framework within which capitalism can activate its advantage as a method of coordination, by a theory of the social genesis and normative justification of preference formation (social psychology and ethics), by a theory of the social institutions of which this framework consists (family, church, state), and by a theory of political compensation for capitalism failure (market failure, the limits of subjectivism, and consideration of substantial life interests).

The necessity of such a framework becomes evident in the dialectic proper to the three structural characteristics of capitalism. In all three characteristics a turnover from quantity into quality and from form into a content is observable.

The unlimited accumulation of private property leads, beyond a certain point of control over a market, to a qualitative jump and to a problem of power. Unlimited pursuit of profits and benefits leads to a turnover into greed, miserliness, and a loss in the wealth of human purposes. The coordination of production and the assignment of social status exclusively by way of market success, that is, successful anticipation of demand and willingness to pay, leads to an exaggerated subjectivism and the neglect of more substantial purposes.

The form of coordination by way of property, maximization of profits, and the market cannot be the content of the social order and individual action, no more so than this form can be abandoned if freedom and efficiency in the economy are to be secured. The theory of capitalism requires a complement from social philosophy and a reminder that reasonable preferences must enter into the coordination. It also needs the reminder that capitalism lives from its ethos of freedom and work, which as a form of economic coordination it alone cannot bring forth and preserve. An ideal of coordination alone cannot do justice to our need for substantial life forms, just as, on the other hand, our need for the recognition of our subjectivity and freedom, in the economy as well, requires the capitalist form of coordination.

Notes

1. Compare from the German neoliberal tradition Röpke (1949) and Rüstow (1945). Recently Bell (1976). The crisis of capitalism is not caused, as Bell shows, by economic inefficiency or the superiority of other systems but by the crisis of cultural and ethical integration in the Western world.

2. This chapter's concept of morality follows the reinterpretation of natural right which has been suggested by Robert Spaemann (1980, pp. 39–40) most recently.

3. Compare Luis de Molina, *De justitia et jure*, Moguntiae (1602), vol. 1 disput.4 n.2: "obligatio juris naturalis oritur a natura objecti"; n.3: "Obligatio oritur a natura rei."

4. For this definition see Kromphardt (1980, p. 38).

5. The degree of embeddedness of the market in social and cultural norms is higher in traditional societies (Polanyi 1971). Compare Dumont (1977), Sahlins (1965), and Tawney (1927).

6. G. Fichte, *Der geschlossene Handelsstaat* (1800). Compare Max Weber (1972, p. 61).

7. For Salin the term *economy* should only be applied to the autonomous economy (1967, p. 2).

8. Ground-breaking work was done by Troeltsche (1923) and recently Johnson (1979).

9. Compare Max Weber (1972, pp. 44–45) with Koslowski (1976, p. 69).

10. See Max Weber (1979).

11. Of course, not to discriminate in prices can be a moral obligation as well.

12. Compare Thomas Aquinas, *Summa theologica* 2-2, q. 77.

13. Hirschman (1977) describes the Christian forerunners of Mandeville who show that the ideological transition to capitalism was gradual.

14. Compare Döllinger and Reusch (1889, p. 4) and Spaemann (1977).

15. Joannes Nider, *Tractatus de contractibus mercatorum*, Paris circa 1495 (Munich: Bayerische Staatsbibliothek, Sign. Nr. 4 1341). "Probabilisme," *Dictionnaire de Théologie Catholique* (Paris 1936) 13, 1, co. 446 calls Nider one of the earliest forerunners of probabilism. Compare P. Koslowski, "Nebenwirkungen," in *Historisches Worterbuch der Philosophie,* vol. 6, by J. Ritter and K. Gründer (Basel, forthcoming).

16. This is as true for the problem of the prohibition of charging interest which can be considered as a special application of restrictions on freedom of contract. The Jesuits, who defended the freedom of the will to do good against the theory of predestination and the necessity of the grace of God for good, also defended the freedom to charge interest for loans against the Dominican position which took the opposite view in both questions (Knoll 1967, pp. 33-4).

17. According to A. Irving Hallowell, a relatively unexplored territory is ethno-metaphysics, that is, the cognitive orientation in a cosmos of people in whatever culture even though the basic premises and principles implied do not happen to be consciously formulated and articulated by the peoples themselves (Foster 1965, p. 293).

18. Compare Otto Brunner (1950) and Koslowski (1976).

19. Compare Singer (1958) and Wagner (1969).

20. Homer *Iliad* 2. 204. Homer's dictum is cited in Aristotle, *Metaphysics Lambda* 1076a. 4-5; and Aristotle again in Thomas Aquinas *Summa theologica* 1 q.103a.3.

21. Cited by Otto Brunner (1950, p. 138).

22. Compare Leo Strauss (1953, p. 8).

23. Compare Thomas Hobbes, *Leviathan,* ed. C.B. Macpherson (London 1968), p. 160: "Felicity is a continuall progresse of the desire, from one object to another; the attaining of the former being still but the way to the latter."

24. Compare H. Grossmann, *Die gesellschaftlichen Grundlagen der mechanistischen Philosophie und die Manufacktur, Zeitschrift für Sozialforschung* 4 (1935) pp. 161-231, reprint (Munich: Kösel, 1970).

25. Compare Sombart (1938, p. 13).

26. Cited by Roscher (1874, p. 481).

27. Cited by Freyer (1921, pp. 14-5). Compare Bonar (1909, p. 221) and Viner (1972, p. 60): "Eighteenth-century British social philosophy was in fact soaked in teleology. I know of no British writer before Bentham who frankly renounced teleology."

28. Katallaxìa, from katallattein (Greek) = to exchange, means an exchange model of the economy. The term *catallactics* meaning theory of an exchange economy was introduced by Archbishop Richard Whately (1787-1863) to replace the term *political economy*. However, Whately was not successful in doing so. The term has been taken up again by the Austrian school of economics by Menger and Gossen, von Mises (1949, p. 233), and von Hayek (1969, p. 112).

29. Compare "Oikonomia," in *A Patristic Greek Lexicon,* ed. G.W. Lampe (Oxford: University Press, 1961).

30. Compare Rowley and Peacock (1975) and Dupuy (1978).

31. See Buchanan (1969, pp. 62-64).

32. Knight asserts, "The assumption that wants or ends are data reduces life to economics and raises again the question with which we started out: Is life all economics or does this view require supplementing by an ethical view of value?" (1935b, pp. 34-5). Similarly, decision theory does not tell the decision maker what to prefer but what to choose under given preferences. According to Segmüller, "Normative decision theory is not an ethics" (1973, p. 325). Thus, decision theory cannot give, in general, effective advice for the selection between alternatives but mostly tells the decision maker only more precisely what he already knew.

33. Plato, *Georgias* 464c.

34. According to Knight, symbolic interactionism "offers much greater possibilities for throwing light on behavior than does the science of behaviorism" (1969, p. 129).

35. See Knight (1947, pp. 4, 372).

36. See W. Röpke (1949, p. 280).

37. Kant had a thorough knowledge of Adam Smith's work and a high esteem for his theory (Koslowski 1981, chap. 5). The structural similarities between Kant's and Smith's theories were stressed and criticized by the German conservative Friedrich Julius Stahl (1802-1861), *Die Philosophie des Rechts,* 5 vols., 1878, reprint (Darmstadt 1963). In vol. 2 p. 100 he sees in Smithonian economics the "analogon of Kantian social philosophy."

38. Plato, *Philebos* 65a,

39. Compare for the value problem Churchman (1961) and on limits of rationality, Simon (1978).

40. Baumol's position falls under Knight's critique: "The striking fact in modern life is the virtually complete separation between spiritual ethics which constitutes its accepted theory of conduct and the unethical, uncriticized notion of efficiency which forms its substitute for a practical ideal, its effective values being accepted unconsciously from tradition or the manipulations of commercial sales managers" (1969, p. 73).

41. Compare Weisskopf (1971).

42. See review article by Albach (1980, p. 3).

43. "Giving the public what it wants usually means corrupting popular taste" (Knight 1969, p. 57).

44. N. Macrae (1981) stresses the possibility of individual life-styles in capitalism.

45. O.V. Nell-Breuning (1974, p. 120), one of the exponents of Catholic social thought in Germany, admits, however, a certain "blindness of theology towards the efficiency and possibilities of markets."

46. See K. v. Fritz, *The Theory of the Mixed Constitution in Antiquity,* (New York: Columbia University Press, 1954), p. 490.

47. The dualism of state and society is a structural constant of European societies since the Greek polis. Compare Koslowski (1982).

48. The excellent books by Hirsch (1976) and Scitovsky (1976) demonstrate the insufficiency of traditional microeconomic theory upon the analysis of preference formation and the satisfaction of needs and, thereby, show the limits of its suitability for policy recommendations, especially for those concerning economic growth policy.

49. See F.W.J. Schelling, *Philosophische Untersuchungen über das Wesen der menschlichen Freiheit* (1809), ed. W. Schulz (Frankfurt, 1975) p. 77; Krings (1980, pp. 15–39).

50. Nell-Breuning aptly criticizes the theory of the market economy in that "more and more, problems are pushed into the so-called data wreath, the framework, and consequently the data wreath ultimately becomes that which is most interesting" (1955, p. 111).

References

Albach H. 1980. "Vertrauen in der ökonomischen Theorie," *Zeitschrift für die gesamte Staatswissenschaft* 136, no. 1; 3.

Alchian, A.A., ed. 1977. *Economic Forces at Work,* pp. 15-36. Indianapolis: Liberty Press.

Alchian, A.A., and Demsetz, H. 1977. "Production, Information Costs and Economic Organization." In *Economic Forces at Work,* edited by A.A. Alchian, pp. 73-110. Indianapolis: Liberty Press.

Arrow, K.J. 1967. "Public and Private Values." In *Human Values and Economic Policy,* edited by S. Hook. New York: New York University Press.

———. 1971. "Political and Economic Evaluation of Social Effects and Externalities." In *Frontiers of Quantitative Economics,* edited by M.D. Intriligator. Amsterdam: North Holland.

Banfield, E.C. 1958. *The Moral Basis of a Backward Society.* Glencoe, Ill.: The Free Press.

Baumol, W.J. 1975. "Business Responsibility and Economic Behavior," In *Altruism, Morality and Economic Theory,* edited by E.S. Phelps. New York: Sage Foundation.

Becker, Gary. 1974. "A Theory of Social Interactions." *Journal of Political Economy* 82.

Bell, D. 1976. *The Cultural Contradictions of Capitalism.* New York: Basic Books.

Böhm-Bawerk, E. v. 1884. *Kapital and Kapitalzins.* Vol. 1., *Geschichte und Kritik der Kapitalzinstheorien.* Innsbruck.

Bonar, J. 1909. *Philosophy and Political Economy in Some of Their Historical Relations.* 1893. Reprint. London: S. Sonnenschein.

Boulding, K.E. 1967. "The Basis of Value Judgements in Economics." In *Human Values and Economic Policy,* edited by S. Hook, pp. 55-72. New York: New York University Press.

_____. 1969. "Economics as a Moral Science." *American Economic Review* 59.

Brunner, Otto. 1950. "Die alteuropäische Ökonomik." *Zeitschrift für Nationalökonomie* 13.

Buchanan, James M. 1954a. "Social Choice, Democracy, and Free Markets." *Journal of Political Economy* 62:114-123.

_____. 1954b. "Individual Choice in Voting an the Market." *Journal of Political Economy* 62:334-343.

_____. 1964. "What Should Economists Do?" *Southern Economic Journal* 30:213-222.

_____. 1965. "Ethical Rules, Expected Values, and Large Numbers." *Ethics* 76:1-13.

_____. 1969. "Is Economics the Science of Choice?" In *Roads to Freedom: Essays in Honour of Friedrich A. von Hayek,* edited by E. Streissler. New York: A.M. Kelly, 1969.

_____. 1978. "Markets, States, and the Extent of Morals." *American Economic Review* 68:364-368.

Buchanan, James M., and Tullock, G. 1974. *The Calculus of Consent.* 5th ed. Ann Arbor: University of Michigan Press.

Churchman, C.W. 1961. *Prediction and Optimal Decision, Philosophical Issues of a Science of Values.* Englewood Cliffs, N.J.: Prentice-Hall.

Coase, R.H. 1960. "The Problem of Social Cost." *Journal of Law & Economics* 3:1-44.

Döllinger, I. v., and Reusch, Fr. H. 1889. *Geschichte der Moralstreitigkeiten in der römisch-katholischen Kirche.* Nördlingen: C.H. Beck.

Dumont, L. 1977. *From Mandeville to Marx: The Genesis and Triumph of Economic Ideology.* Chicago: University of Chicago Press.

Dupuy, J.P. 1978. "L'économie de la morale, ou la morale de l'économie." *Revue d'Économie Politique* 88:404-439.

Foster, G.M. 1965. "Peasant Society and the Image of Limited Good." *American Anthropologist* 67:293.

Freyer, H. 1966. *Die Bewertung der Wirtschaft im philosophischen Denken des 19. Jahrhunderts.* 1921. Reprint. Hildescheim: Olms.

Hayek, F.A. von. 1968. *Der Wettbewerb als Entdeckungsverfahren.* Kiel: Institut für Weltwirtschaft.

————. 1969. *Freiberger Studien.* Walter Eucken Institut (Hrsg.), Wirtschaftswissenschaftliche und wirtschaftsrechtliche Untersuchungen 5. Tubingen: J.C.B. Mohr (Paul Sieback).

————. 1977. *Drei Vorlesungen über Demokratie, Gerechtigkeit und Sozialismus.* Walter Eucken Institut (Hrsg.), Vorträge and Aufsätze 63, Tubingen: J.C.B. Mohr (Paul Siebeck).

Hegel, Georg Wilhelm Friedrich. *Philosophy of Right,* translated with notes by T.M. Knox. Chicago, Ill.: Encyclopedia Britannica.

Hirsch F. 1976. *Social Limits to Growth.* Cambridge, Mass.: Harvard University Press.

Hirschman, A.O. 1970. *Exit, Voice, and Loyalty: Responses to Decline in Firms, Organizations, and States.* Cambridge, Mass.: Harvard University Press.

————. 1977. *The Passions and the Interests: Political Arguments for Capitalism before its Triumph.* Princeton, N.J.: Princeton University Press.

Hirshleifer, J. 1978. "Competition, Cooperation, and Conflict in Economics and Biology." *American Economic Review* 68:238.

Hook, S., ed. 1967. *Human Values and Economic Policy.* New York: New York University Press.

Hutchison, T.W. 1979. "Notes on the Effects of Economic Ideas on Policy: The Example of the German Social Market Economy." *ZgG* 135:433.

Johnson, P. 1979. "Is there a Moral Basis for Capitalism? Dissenting Thoughts in a Collectivist Age." *Encounter* (October):15-25.

Jünger, E. 1952. *Der Waldgang.* Frankfurt: Klostermann.

Kant, I. 1898. *Critisme of Practical Reason,* p. 368. London: Longmans, Green & Co.

Knight, F.H. 1947. *Freedom and Reform.* New York: Harper.

————. 1966. "Abstract Economics as Absolute Ethics." *Ethics* 76:163-177.

————. 1969. *The Ethics of Competition and Other Essays.* 1935. Reprint. Freeport, N.Y.: Books for Libraries Press.

Knoll, A.M. 1967. *Zins und Gnade. Zur Zins-und Gnadenkontroverse der Dominikaner and Jesuiten, Lutheraner and Calvinet.* Neuwied: Luchterhand.

Koslowski, Peter I. 1979a. "Haus and Geld, Zur aristotelischen Unterscheidung von Politik, Ökonomik and Chrematistik." *Philosophisches Jahrbuch* 86: 60-83.

————. 1979b. *Zum Verhältnis von Polis and Oikos bei Aristoteles, Politik und Ökonomie bei Aristoteles.* 2d ed. Straubing: Donau.

_____. 1982. *Gesellschaft und Staat. Ein unvermeidlicher Dualismus.* Stuttgart: Klett-Cotta.

Krings, H. 1980. *System und Freiheit. Gesammelte Aufsätze.* Frieburg: Alber.

Kromphardt, J. 1980. *Konzeptionen und Analysen des Kapitalismus.* Göttingen: Vandenhoeck.

Luhmann, N. 1977. *Zweckbegriff und Systemrationalität. Über die Funktion von Zwecken in sozialen Systemen.* 2d ed. Frankfurt: Suhrkamp.

MacPherson, C.B. 1962. *The Political Theory of Possessive Individualism: Hobbes to Locke.* London: Oxford University Press.

Macrae, N. 1981. "Für eine Welt individueller Lebensstile." In *Fortschritt ohne Maß? Eine Ortsbestimmung der wissenschaftlich-technischen Zivilisation,* edited by R. Löw, P. Koslowski, and P. Kreuzer, pp. 213-233. Munich: Piper.

Marshak, J. 1974. *Economic Information, Decision and Prediction,* vol. 2, pp. 193-199. Dordrecht: Reidel.

Mises, L. von. 1949. *Human Action.* New Haven: Yale University Press.

Nell-Breuning, O. v. 1955. "Noeliberalismus und Katholische Soziallehre." In *Der Christ und die soziale Marktwirtschaft,* edited by P.M. Boarmann. Stuttgart: Kohlhammer.

_____. 1974. *Kapitalismus–kritisch betrachtet.* Frieburg: Herder.

Norman, Edward R. 1979. "Denigration of Capitalism." In *The Denignation Capitalism: Six Points of View,* edited by M. Novack, pp. 7-23. Washington, D.C.: American Enterprise Institute.

Novack, M., ed. 1979. *The Denigration of Capitalism: Six Points of View.* Washington, D.C.: American Enterprise Institute.

Nozick, R. 1974. *Anarchy, State, and Utopia.* Oxford: Basil Blackwell.

Passow, R. 1927. *Kapitalismus, Eine begrifflich-terminologische Studie.* Jena: Fisher.

Phelps, E.S., ed. 1975. *Altruism, Morality and Economic Theory.* New York: Sage Foundation.

Polanyi, K. 1971. *Primitive, Archaic and Modern Economies.* Boston: Beacon Press.

Posner, R.A. 1977. *Economic Analysis of Law.* Boston: Little, Brown.

Röpke, J. 1970. *Primitive Wirtschaft, Kulturwandel und die Diffusion von Neuerungen.* Tubingen: J.C.B. Mohr (Paul Siebeck).

Röpke, W. 1949. *Civita Humana: Grundfragen der Gesellschafts-und Wirtschaftsreform.* Erlenback-Zurich: Rentsch.

Roscher, W. 1874. *Geschichte der Nationalökonomik in Deutschland.* Munich: Oldenbourg.

Rowley, C.K., and Peacock, A.T. 1975. *Welfare Economics: A Liberal Restatement.* London: Martin Robertson.

Rüstow, A. 1945. *Das Versagen des Wirtschaftsliberalismus als religions-geschichtliches Problem.* Zurich and New York: Europa Verlag.

Sahlins, M.D. 1965. "Exchange-Value and the Diplomacy of Primitive Trade." In *Essays in Economic Anthropology: Dedicated to the Memory of Karl Polanyi.* Seattle: University of Washington Press.

Salin, Edgar. 1967. *Politische Ökonomie.* Tubingen: J.C.B. Mohr (Paul Siebeck).

Sauermann, Heinz, ed. 1978. *Bargaining Behavior,* p. 383. Tubingen: Mohr.

Schall, J.V. 1979. "Religion and the Demise of Capitalism." In *The Denigration of Capitalism: Six Points of View,* edited by M. Novack, pp. 32–38. Washington, D.C.: American Enterprise Institute.

Scheler, Max. 1966. *Der Formalismus in der Ethik und die materiale Wertethik.* 5th ed. Bern: Frankke.

Schumacher, E.F. 1973. *Small Is Beautiful.* London: Blond and Briggs.

Schumpeter, J.A. 1955. *History of Economic Analysis.* 5th ed. London: Allen & Unwin.

Scitovsky, T. 1976. *The Joyless Economy.* London: Oxford University Press.

Sen, A. 1967. "Isolation, Assurance and the Social Rate of Discount." *Quarterly Journal of Economics* 81:112–124.

———. 1973. *On Economic Inequality.* Oxford: Clarendon Press.

Shackle, G.L.S. 1972. *Epistemics and Economics: A Critique of Economic Doctrines.* Cambridge: At the University Press.

Simon, H.A. 1978. "Rationality as Process and as Product of Thought." *American Economic Review* 68:1–15.

Singer, K. 1958. "Oikonomia: An Inquiry into Beginnings of Economic Thought and Language." *Kyklos* 11:29–57.

Sombart, W. 1938. *Weltanschauung, Wissenschaft und Wirtschaft.* Berlin: Buchholz and Weisswange.

Spaemann, Robert. 1977. "Nebenwirkungen als moralisches Problem." In *Zur Kirtik der politischen Utopie,* edited by R. Spaemann. Stuttgart: Klett.

———. 1980. "Christentum und Kernkraft. Ethische Aspekte der Energie politik." *Die Politische Meinung* 192.

Stegmüller, W. 1973. *Probleme und Resultate der Wissenschaftstheorie und Analytischen Philosophie. Personelle und statistische Wahrscheinlichkeit. I. Halbbd.: Personelle Wahrscheinlichkeit und rationale Entscheidung.* Berlin: Springer.

Strauss, L. 1953. *Natural Right and History.* Chicago: University of Chicago Press.

Tawney, R.H. 1937. *Religion and the Rise of Capitalism.* 2d ed. London: John Murray.

Troeltsche, E. 1923. *Die Soziallehren der christlichen Kirchen und Gruppen.* Tubingen: J.C.B. Mohr (Paul Siebeck).

Viner, J. 1972. *The Role of Providence in the Social Order: An Essay in Intellectual History.* Philadelphia: American Philosophical Society.

Wagner, F. 1969. *Das Bild der frühen Ökonomik.* Salzburg: Stifterbibliothek.

Weber, Max. 1972. *Wirtschaft und Gesellschaft.* 5th ed. Tubingen: J.C.B. Mohr (Paul Siebeck).

_____. 1979. *Die protestantische Ethik und der Geist des Kapitalismus.* Gütersloh: Mohn.

Weisskopf, W.A. 1971. *Alienation and Economics.* New York: Dutton.

Williamson, O.E. 1977. "Firms and Markets." In *Modern Economic Thought,* edited by S. Weintraub. Philadelphia: University of Pennsylvania Press.

_____. 1981. "The Modern Corporation: Origins, Evolution, Attributes." *Journal of Economic Literature* 19:1537–1570.

5 Constitutional Contract in Capitalism

James M. Buchanan

This chapter will introduce four separate elements to construct an argument that will both clarify some of the issues raised under the rubric *the morality of capitalism* and offer some suggestions concerning the potential for deriving an acceptable morality. The separate and apparently disparate elements are the following:

1. Peter I. Koslowski's stress on the conflict between the autonomy of the individual in capitalistic economies and what he calls *value rationality* in society;
2. Michael Polanyi's diagnosis of the modern historical experience as characterized by *moral inversion*;
3. Frank Knight's emphasis on the significance of the *relatively absolute absolutes,* a conception that is indispensable in all discussions on topics such as those in this book;
4. Finally, my own often repeated emphasis on the necessity of making a distinction in one's thinking between the *constitutional* level of discourse, evaluation, or choice and the *postconstitutional* level.[1]

In chapter 4, Peter I. Koslowski is surely correct when he suggests that we (the set of persons in an existing capitalistic or quasi-capitalistic order) are unwilling to accept fully the individualistic autonomy of the free market (more inclusively, the free society) on moral grounds. We are unwilling to place an explicit positive evaluation on the pattern of results that catallactic interaction generates. This reluctance to attribute what one might call *moral worthiness* to the free economy does not stem either from some failure to value the *liberty* of individual choice that only the capitalistic order allows or from some lack of interest in attainment of the highest possible satisfaction of whatever preferences that may exist (*efficiency*). Morally, one rejects the autonomy of individual choice that the market embodies because one assigns to the market the wholly inappropriate task of generating morally satisfying sets of preferences. Koslowsky argues, quite rightly, that a theory of the formation of preferences is logically prior to a theory of the allocation of means to meet those preferences. He goes on to challenge the moral status of the Pareto norm even if one disregards the theory problem of the initial distribution of endowments. The point is that if a distribution of endowments is given, and if preferences are what they are, then there is positive moral content in the Pareto norm for the elementary reason that the Pareto optimum describes the end-state to which freedom of individual choice will lead in the absence of arbitrary constraints. In Koslowski's terms, however, one expects the normative theory of allocation to include a normative theory of preference formation. As Frank Knight was so fond of emphasizing, what one really wants is to have better preferences.

Knight's suggestion here seems to have empirical support, based both on introspection and external observation. It is, nonetheless, paradoxical in one sense. One is unable to define which set of preferences is better. Having long since rejected the truths of revealed religion, one cannot construct universally acceptable criteria for betterness through the use of scientific-rationalistic procedures. One wants what he cannot define, yet somehow one knows that that which one wants is there behind the curtain that divides present from future. Why, then, does one want better preferences?

At this point, Polanyi's notion of moral inversion becomes relevant;[2] Polanyi suggests that modern man is characterized by an excess of moral fervor that seeks outlets. With the erosion of emphasis upon personal salvation in a quest for life hereafter, there came in consequence a necessary decline in the internalization of morals. Individual morality was no longer instrumentally required for individually meaningful purposes. The rationality of science, carried to its limits, suggested that there were no absolute values upon which moral emphasis might be centered. Cannibalism was placed on all fours with Franciscan charity. In this modern environment, persons who seek outlets for their moral passions and who possess no powers of discrimination become highly vulnerable to exploitation by persuasive leaders who promote the varying final solutions of this century. Polanyi holds out the hope that as the post-Christian residues of moral passion dissipate, modern man may become more willing to accept the autonomous order of the free society.

Polanyi's hypothesis is an interesting one with perhaps some explanatory value. But it is doubtful whether one can place much hope in the improvement that it offers. The Polanyi hypothesis may explain the behavior and the success of some of the zealots of this century (the terror about which Koslowski speaks), and it may possibly suggest that the ranks of the zealots may be expected to thin a bit. But it seems highly unlikely that man in the late twentieth and early twenty-first centuries will cease and desist in his moral condemnations of the market order and that he will at least attain some position of moral neutrality with respect to the freedom of choice that the market embodies. Can one expect one's children and grandchildren to accept that pushpin is as good as poetry?

There is, however, a basis in Polanyi's conception that may be turned to constructive purpose. If one agrees that the inherent moral urgings of man will neither return to the inward-seeking soul of medieval Europe nor fade into moral quiescence, the challenge to the social philosopher stands clear. This challenge is to design institutional structures that will channel these moral urgings so as to satisfy two objectives simultaneously. First, the outlets must be such that those persons whose whole being exists in their actual or imagined efforts toward furtherance of a better world can experience fulfillment without frustration in some pragmatically limited sense. Second, the very real values of liberty and efficiency that the autonomous order of capitalistic constitutional democracy guarantees must be preserved.

To make progress, one must first, at the level of discourse among academic philosophers (broadly defined), come to accept and to understand as relevant the basic distinction between the two levels of choice toward which the rhetoric might be directed, that is, the constitutional and the postconstitutional, to which I have earlier, and elsewhere, referred. (A long-continuing personal frustration for me has been the apparent inability of obviously competent social scientists, who may share my basic values in one sense, literally to understand what I am talking about when I stress the constitutional-postconstitutional distinction.)

What does this distinction, which may admittedly be relevant for political reform, have to do with the morality of capitalism and with prospects for resolving or reducing the moral conflict between the autonomous individualism of the market and the moral urgings of men to live in a better society? The adoption of the *constitutional attitude* can be of major assistance in any discussion of preference formation. At this point, the Knightian emphasis on the relatively absolute absolutes comes to be of critical importance. The normative theory of allocation embodies preferences as they exist, and within this theory these preferences are to be taken as relatively absolute. Relevant choices within this normative setting are analogous to *postconstitutional* choices; existing preferences are given in the environment. Within this normative context, pushpin (rock music, Harold Robbins fiction, TV situation comedy) is as good as poetry (classical music or Shakespeare).

At a second or constitutional level of discourse, however, existent sets of preferences need not be accepted, and, indeed, one of the aims of such discourse becomes effective criticism of such preferences with some view toward improvement through appropriate institutional change. Preferences for pushpin are not so good as preferences for poetry, and the social philosopher-cum-scientist has as one of his central tasks the design of constitutional-institutional structure that will promote the emergence of better preferences (for example, poetry). His normative effort is grossly, and sometimes tragically, misdirected if he fails to understand the appropriate level of choice for his endeavor and if as a consequence he seeks by resorting to the coercive agency of the state to impose his own preferences on others. The moralist who stands outraged at the tastes of his fellows must learn to vent his anger where it belongs on the institutions that generate the preferences and notably the educational establishment, rather than on those of the market economy which are, or may be, wholly neutral between rock and classical music.

Properly conceived and understood, the discussion-debate over the preferred set of constraining institutions within which individuals are to be allowed to exercise their free choices may be characterized by intense disagreement. As noted, the activity cannot be conceived as a search for a single truth, waiting to be discovered. However, because no one can fully define just what better preferences look like, and because the direct objects for adjustment are quasi-permanent institutional parameters, self-interest of the narrow sort will not dominate the behavior of participants in the discussion. Important elements of some Rawls-like veil of ignorance are necessarily present. The relegation of narrow self-interest to a subsidiary role will tend to insure that agreement or consensus is more readily attainable.

The concern here, however, is not whether or not agreement can or cannot be reached on the set of institutions within which the preferences of future persons (including oneself) will be allowed to emerge. The point is, rather, that it is at this level and this level only that the exercise of moral passion must be practiced. This level of discourse, that which has the normative theory of preference formation as its central focus, can embody severe criticisms of the preferences that are observed. The moralist who advances such criticisms, however, can accept at the same time the latter preferences as they are as relatively absolute absolutes that are to be accorded existential status in the normative theory of allocation.

This is not to suggest that the shift in attitudes outlined will be easy to accomplish or if once accomplished, easy to maintain. In a game-theory analogy, the challenge seems relatively manageable. It seems reasonable to expect that persons might continue to play a game within defined rules while, at the same time, bringing critical judgment to bear on changing these rules. In other words, they might continue to work to promote desired objectives (continue to seek efficient postconstitutional policy changes) within a defined constitutional structure while simultaneously seeking to promote changes in the structure itself, changes that promise to open up some preferred set of postconstitutional options.

In effect, the existing preferences are interpreted at least indirectly as a part of the rules of the game in which everyone is engaged. If the game is to continue at all, one must learn to accept these rules and play within them as effectively as possible. Rules are not absolutes; they are subject to criticism, comparative evaluation, and possible change. In this context, preferences can be shifted but only through a long-term process of institutional adjustment.

It is important to acknowledge the optimistic Enlightenment folly for what it was. If left wholly unconstrained, men will not seek only the good, the true, and the beautiful. It is not so easy to escape personal responsibility for the order of society. The free society that is to be worth living in must be constitutionally constructed.

Notes

1. Only after I had developed an outline of a theme for these remarks did I recall that many aspects of the same argument are contained in an earlier paper

that concentrates on a dispute between Michael Polanyi and Frank Knight. See my "Politics and Science," *Ethics* 77(July 1967):303-310. Reprinted in James M. Buchanan, *Freedom in Constitutional Contract* (College Station: Texas A&M University Press, 1978), pp. 64-77.

2. Polanyi's conception is discussed in Michael Polanyi and Harry Prosch, *Meaning* (Chicago: University of Chicago Press, 1975).

Libertarian Evolutionism and Contractarian Constitutionalism

Viktor Vanberg

In reading F.A. von Hayek's *Constitution of Liberty* (1961) and his *Law, Legislation, and Liberty* (1979, vol. 3) and James M. Buchanan's *Freedom in Constitutional Contract* (1978), one may feel a bit uncertain about how the conceptions of these two leading scholars on the social foundations of capitalism may be related to one another. Although both scholars apparently start from similar theoretical premises—both are methodological individualists in a strict sense—and both agree in their criticism of certain developments in Western democracies as well as in their search for effective constitutional limits to the growth of government, they seem to take quite different conceptions in certain respects. Buchanan refers to these differences when he classifies Hayek as an evolutionist and in contrast characterizes his own position as a contractarian one, that may possibly fall under Hayek's verdict of rationalist constructivism.

The purpose of this chapter is to have a closer look at this striking mixture of agreement and dissent in Hayek's and Buchanan's respective theoretical and philosophical conceptions of capitalism. The concept of *evolution,* which is used by Hayek to denote different conceptions that though being interrelated can and ought to be separated, will be examined first. Thereafter the concept of *constructivist rationalism* under which Hayek also subsumes different notions that may be separated corresponding to the different notions of evolution will be considered. After this analysis the question of whether Buchanan's *contractarian* position is in fact in conflict with the position taken by Hayek, or whether, on the contrary, both positions are reconcilable and should be reconciled if one wants to get an internally consistent libertarian prospect for constitutional reforms will be examined.

Hayek on Evolution

In Hayek's writings there is a close connection between the idea of an evolutionary process and the concept of a spontaneous or self-generating order, a connection Hayek emphasizes in speaking of "the twin concepts of evolution and spontaneous order" (1979, p. 158). It is certainly not necessary here to elaborate Hayek's well-known arguments on the formation of a spontaneous order. The only point to stress here is that there are two different notions involved when the emergence of a spontaneous or grown order is characterized by Hayek as the unintended outcome of an evolutionary process.

The first notion is that if the behavior of men is governed by certain general or abstract rules, the separate actions of the individuals will produce an overall order as an unintended evolutionary outcome. The second notion is that the abstract rules which serve the formation of a spontaneous order are themselves the unintended product of an evolutionary process. The distinction between these two notions is important with respect to the arguments Hayek uses to characterize the process of evolution and to substantiate his warnings against deliberate interventions into the spontaneous process.

Since the arguments relevant to the first notion are well known from discussions on the properties of market processes, a few remarks may be sufficient here. The basic argument in this notion is that a spontaneous order is brought about by processes of mutual adaptation among the separate individuals, and from this argument it is concluded that in a spontaneous order far more knowledge will be used than could be ever used in deliberate arrangements because the individuals are free—restricted by general rules only—to adapt themselves to particular circumstances known only to them. When the formation of a spontaneous order is thus characterized as an evolutionary process, this primarily refers to the fact that it is "a process the outcome of which will depend on a very large number of particular facts, far too numerous for us to know in their entirety" (Hayek 1973, p. 23-24).

According to the second notion, which is of more relevance to the purpose of this chapter, the crucial argument is that "most of the rules which do govern existing society are . . . the product of a process of evolution in the course of which much more experience and knowledge has been precipitated in them than any one person can fully know (Hayek 1967, p. 92). This argument is based upon the idea that the elimination and selection of rules and institutions is an evolutionary process in being "guided not by reason but by success" (Hayek 1979, p. 166). It is a process involving competition among organized and unorganized groups as well as competition among individuals (Hayek 1960, p. 37). In a competitive process, it is supposed that those rules and institutions have prevailed which made a group of people successful and which enabled that group in which they had arisen to prevail over others (Hayek 1973, p. 917).[1] When the idea of "the prevalance of the more effective institutions in a process of competition" is thus closely connected with the conception of group selection (Hayek 1979, p. 155, 202), this, of course, does not mean that—as in biology—conceptions such as natural selection, and so forth, shall be applied here. In social evolution, as Hayek emphasizes, "the decisive factor is not the selection of the physical and inheritable properties of the individuals but the selection by imitation of successful institutions and habits," that is, social evolution primarily is a matter of learning and imitation (1960, p. 59). When in the light of the two notions of evolution distinguished before one analyzes Hayek's arguments on what he calls constructivistic rationalism, it becomes apparent that an analogous distinction among different notions of constructivistic rationalism may be made.

Hayek on Constructivist Rationalism

Under the head of constructivist rationalist Hayek criticizes, on the one side, the idea of a deliberate organization of society in the sense of an organization directing the activities of the individuals (not by general rules but) by commands in order to achieve certain desired results. According to this notion of constructivist rationalism, the "activities of all should be centrally directed according to a single plan laid down by a central authority" (Hayek 1967, p. 82). The claim to "achieve a desirable order of society by concretely arranging all its parts in full knowledge of all the relevant facts" by necessity destroys, as Hayek emphasizes, the creative forces of the spontaneous order of society by transforming it "into a single organization built and directed according to a single plan" (Hayek 1967, p. 82; 1960, p. 37). This kind of constructivist rationalism apparently is related to the first of the two notions of evolution distinguished before. As Hayek argues, the characteristic error of such a constructivist rationalism is its "fiction that all the relevant facts are know to some mind" and its failure to recognize the "impossibility of anyone taking conscious account of all the particular facts, which enter into the order of society" (Hayek 1973, pp. 13-14). In this respect the crucial argument against deliberate interventions into the evolutionary process of the formation of a spontaneous order is that if each individual is free to act on his particular knowledge "more knowledge is utilized than . . . is possible to synthesize intellectually" (Hayek 1960, p. 30).[2]

On the other side, Hayek also criticizes under the head of constructivist rationalism the idea of a deliberate construction of the rules and institutions which govern the spontaneous order of society. This criticism, which apparently refers to the second of the before mentioned two notions of evolution, is an attack on design theories of social rules and institutions which, as Hayek argues, "stand in irreconcilable conflict with all we know about the evolution of law and most other human institutions" (1973, p. 73).[3] Constructivist rationalism in this sense is to be understood as labeling "a conception which assumes that all social institutions are, and ought to be, the product of deliberate design" (Hayek 1973, p. 5).[4] It is obvious that with respect to the conception of the evolution of rules and institutions the criticism of deliberate interventions into the evolutionary process cannot be based upon the same arguments which are used to criticize that notion of constructivist rationalism that was analyzed before, that is, deliberate interventions cannot be censured as being in irreconcilable conflict with the fundamental principles of a spontaneous order. Since, as Hayek states,

> while the rules on which a spontaneous order rests, may also be of spontaneous origin, this need not always be the case . . . and it is at least conceivable that the formation of a spontaneous order relies entirely on rules that were deliberately made. The spontaneous character of the resulting order must therefore be distinguished from the

spontaneous origin of the rules on which it rests, and it is possible that an order which would still have to be described as spontaneous rests on rules which are entirely the result of deliberate design (1973, p. 45).

Accordingly, in his criticism of constructivist rationalism with respect to rules and institutions, Hayek refers to a different kind of argument. His central objection to this version of constructivist rationalism is, that "no single human intelligence is capable of inventing the most appropriate abstract rules because those rules which have evolved in the process of growth of society embody the experience of many more trials and errors than any individual mind could acquire" (1967, p. 88). Hence, Hayek argues, "it is unlikely that any individual would succeed in rationally constructing rules which would be more effective for their purpose than those which have been gradually evolved" (1960, p. 66).

When Hayek thus refers to the cumulative embodiment of experience in spontaneously grown rules and institutions as an argument against constructivist rationalism, this apparently does not mean, however, that as an evolutionist he wants to ban any deliberate creation and modification of rules and institutions (1960, p. 33).[5] Though his emphasis is on spontaneous evolution, Hayek nevertheless admits that at least in modern societies part of the rules which people observe are in fact—and usefully can be—deliberately designed. Although there are rules, notably rules of morals and custom, that may appropriately be regarded as the spontaneous outcome of an evolutionary process, it is obvious that there also are rules, notably rules of law, which are subject to deliberate design since they are shaped and altered by legislation (see Hayek 1973, p. 46). Hence, according to Hayek, one faces the "important question of which of these rules of individual action can be deliberately and profitably altered, and which are likely to evolve gradually with or without such deliberate collective decisions as legislation involves" (1967, p. 72). As Hayek admits, the rules on which the formation of a spontaneous order rests not only may possibly be improved by legislation,[6] it may even be necessary deliberately to correct by legislation spontaneous processes of growth leading in very undesirable directions.[7]

Accordingly, what Hayek's criticism of constructivist rationalism with respect to rules and institutions in fact amount to is a refusal of the idea of a total reconstruction of the entire system of rules on which spontaneous order rests. His true argument seems to be that an improvement of these rules is more likely to be brought about by an experimental, piecemeal process than by a total rebuilding of the whole system and "that, although we must always strive to improve our institutions, we can never aim to remake them as a whole" (Hayek 1960, p. 63).[8]

From this analysis notably two conclusions can be drawn. First, in opposing the evolutionist and the constructivist-rationalist conceptions of rules and institutions Hayek advances an assymmetric antithesis. Although the constructivist-rationalist conception is identified with the rather specific assumption that all social institutions are and ought to be the product of deliberate design, the evolutionist conception is identified with the comparatively unspecific proposition that some rules and institutions are of spontaneous origin,[9] and that the process of spontaneous growth may sometimes produce institutions that are most beneficial to the functioning of society.[10] Second, the evolutionist conception obviously has its focus in the analysis of processes by which social outcomes are brought about as the unintended combined results of separate individual choices. In legislation, however, one faces processes of (deliberate) social choices, and hence the question arises whether the evolutionist conception may also be helpful in analyzing these processes, or whether alternative theoretical approaches may be more appropriate here. It is this question which is of crucial importance for the issue of constitutional reform on which the following discussion will concentrate.

Constructivist Rationalism and Constitutional Rules

The previous discussion was intended to elaborate the precise meaning that the concept of *constructivist raitonalism* has with respect to rules and institutions. Before conclusions can be drawn from this discussion for the issue of constitutional reforms, it is first necessary to make a further distinction, namely, that between rules of just conduct and constitutional rules. Since the previous discussion tacitly was confined to rules of just conduct, the arguments quoted there cannot simply be transferred to constitutional rules because these are of a different character. In contrast to the "universal rules of just conduct which form the basis of the spontaneous order of society at large" by limiting "the range of permitted action" (Hayek 1973, pp. 125, 127), the rules comprised in a constitution are "chiefly concerned with the organization of government and the allocation of the different powers to the various parts of this organization" (Hayek 1979, p. 37).[11] These constitutional rules are rules of organization and rules that concern the allocation and limitation of the powers of government (Hayek 1979, p. 134).[12] Although the rules of just conduct did not need to be deliberately made, government, on the other hand, is a deliberate contrivance which requires its own distinct rules to determine its structure, aims, and functions (Hayek 1973, p. 24).[13] Thus, according to Hayek, "there always existed of necessity an authority which had power to make . . . the rules of the organization of government," that is, constitutional rules have always been subject to deliberate construction (1973, p. 90).

This implies, however, that when applied to constitutional rules the concepts of evolution and of constructivist rationalism necessarily must have a meaning different from that elaborated in the previous discussion. With respect to the general rules of conduct the idea of an evolutionary process centers around the notion of a decentralized competitive process in which it is determined by separate individual choices which rules of conduct will prevail. This notion is articulated, for instance, when Hayek argues that most "steps in the evolution of culture were made possible by some individuals breaking some traditional rules and practicing new forms of conduct." and that the innovations of these rule-breakers were successful to the same degree as they were adopted by their fellow-citizens (1979, p. 161).[14] Obviously this notion of a process in which the selection of rules in a matter of individual choices is less appropriate with regard to the rules of law, which are subject to the deliberate collective decisions of legislation than it is with regard to the rules of morals and custom (Hayek 1967, p. 72).[15] It is evidently inappropriate with regard to constitutional rules which of necessity are a matter of social choice. They do not spread slowly over the community; they can be changed only discontinuously and for all at the same time.

Accordingly, what with regard to constitutional rules Hayek criticizes as constructivist rationalism primarily seems not to be a specific view of constitution making but a conception refusing the ideal of a limiting constitution. Since, according to Hayek, constitutionalism means limited government," this kind of constructivist rationalism may be labeled as *anticonstitutionalism* (1973, p. 1). It is obviously such a conception that Hayek has in mind when he blames constructivist rationalism for refusing to submit to the discipline of abstract rules, and for believing in some single unlimited supreme power (1973, p. 34; 1979, p. 129).[16]

Though his criticism of rationalist constructivism obviously has no direct bearing on the issue of a deliberate designing of a constitution, Hayek seems to be somewhat ambivalent at this point. Thus he criticizes the rationalist conceptions of the social contract, and he seems to subsume the whole contractarian tradition under the label of constructivist rationalism while at the same time he estimates the U.S. Constitution as a constitution of liberty although it obviously is a product of deliberate design.[17] Hayek seems to feel a need to reconcile his criticism of constructivist rationalism and his appreciation of the U.S. Constituion when he states, "The Americans were very conscious of the unique nature of their undertaking . . . they were guided by a spirit of rationalism, a desire for deliberate construction and pragmatic procedure closer to what we have called the French tradition than to the British" (1960, p. 183). However, as Hayek proceeds in order to accommodate this picture to his conception, he points out that what "new discoveries the federal Constitution contained either resulted from the application of traditional principles to particular problems or emerged as only dimly perceived consequences of general ideas" (1960, p. 184).[18]

In focusing his attention on the antithesis of evolutionism versus constructivist rationalism Hayek seems to have difficulties in finding in his own conception a consistent place for deliberate constitutional designs and reforms. This question will be taken up again after a discussion of the contractarian constitutionalism which Buchanan proposes as an alternative conception to Hayek's evolutionism.

Buchanan's Criticism of Evolutionism:
The Contractarian Alternative

As the previous discussion was intended to show, Hayek's characterization of an evolutionist conception, on the one side, and of a constructivist-rationalist, one on the other, is in fact not a homogenous notion but a notion subsuming a set of propositions and arguments which indeed are intellectually interrelated but which have quite different implications. Notwithstanding these different implications, however, there seems to be a basic presumption underlying Hayek's arguments that may perhaps be adequately labeled as *evolutionist optimism.* By his arguments Hayek primarily directs attention to the fact that the spontaneous interactions of individuals, separately striving for private aims, unintendedly may bring about desirable social results. The crucial idea in this context is that in a spontaneous process more information and more knowledge can be utilized than is possible in a deliberate arrangement. This information-argument is the common core of the previously mentioned two notions included in Hayek's conception of an evolutionary process: (1) his notion of the decentralized utilization of knowledge in a spontaneous order and (2) his notion of the cumulative embodiment of experience in spontaneously grown institutions.

In focusing attention on arguments which give reason to the presumption that the outcomes of spontaneous-evolutionary processes may be socially desirable, Hayek seems to be relatively uninterested in the issue of how the possible emergence of socially desirable outcomes may be dealt with theoretically and practically. He certainly concedes that his considerations on the favorable features of evolutionary processes do not prove that all the sets of moral beliefs which have evolved in a society will be beneficial and that some habits and institutions may be "retained long after they have outlived their usefulness and even when they have become more an obstacle than a help" (1960, p. 26, 67). But the emphasis in Hayek's argument clearly is on the possibly beneficial outcomes of evolutionary processes and on the possibly injurious outcomes of deliberate arrangements and collective decision processes, that is, his argument primarily rests on a presumption which is made explicit in the following statement:

We have no ground for crediting majority decisions with that higher, superindividual wisdom which, in a certain sense, the products of spontaneous social growth may possess. . . . If by "social process" we mean the gradual evolution which produces better solutions than deliberate design, the imposition of the will of the majority can hardly be regarded as such. The latter differs radically from that free growth from which custom and institutions merge, because its coercive, monopolistic, and exclusive character destroys the self-correcting forces which bring it about in a free society that mistaken efforts will be abandoned and the successful ones prevail (1960, p. 110).[19]

It is in explicit opposition to Hayek's evolutionist optimism that Buchanan states: "I have no faith in the efficacy of social evolutionary process. The institutions that survive and prosper need not be those that maximize man's potential. Evolution may produce social dilemma as readily as social paradise" (1975, p. 167).[20] According to Buchanan, a basic shortcoming in Hayek's evolutionist conception is that in "his specific attribution of invisible-hand characteristics to the evolution of legal institutions Hayek seems to have failed to separate properly the positive and the normative implications" of the principle of spontaneous order or—what is synonymous—the invisible-hand principle (1977, p. 31).[21] As an explanatory approach, the invisible-hand principle is, as Buchanan argues, fully neutral with respect to the social efficiency or inefficiency of the spontaneously produced results, that is, "invisible-hand explanations may be applicable to orders that are clearly recognized to be undesirable as to those that are recognized to be desirable" (1977, p. 28). Accordingly, the fact that an institution may adequately be explained as "produced by the operation of the invisible hand, by the independent and separate utility maximizing behaviour of persons" does per se not imply that it is socially efficient (Buchanan 1977, p. 30).

Buchanan finds Hayek's argument misleading in suggesting that those institutions which have evolved spontaneously embody efficiency attributes and that deliberate constructions tend to be inefficient (1977, p. 32).[22] If, however, as Buchanan stresses, "an explanation of the results by the operation of invisible hand responses need not carry with it normative overtones" then the question is how criteria for evaluating existing law and institutions can be introduced (1977, p. 32). While Hayek, beyond his normative inferences from the evolutionist perspective, seems to offer no explicit criteria for evaluation, it is Buchanan's central thesis that in order to find such criteria with an individualist framework one has to rely on something like a contractarian position.[23] According to such a position, one "may evaluate any element of the existing legal structure in terms of its possible consistency with that which might emerge from a genuine social contract among all persons who are involved in the interaction" (Buchanan 1977, p. 33). On the basis of such as if contractarian criteria the elements of the existing legal-institutional structure can be evaluated and proposals for reform can be advanced, irrespective of whether the respective elements historically have been brought about by spontaneous growth or by deliberate design.[24] As Buchanan stresses, though in "a positive empirical sense, many of our social-legal institutions have grown independently of design and intent," in a contractarian perspective one "must look on *all* institutions as potentially improvable," and "earnings against unnecessary and ill-timed interferences with legal institutions should not extend to the point of inhibiting us against efforts of improvement" (1977, pp. 38, 31).

When on the basis of as if contractarian criteria elements of the legal-institutional structure may be provisionally classified as inefficient, "proposals for change can be, and should be, constructed and then presented for possible approval or disapproval by the members of the relevant public, the participants in the intereaction" (Buchanan 1977, p. 34). With respect to the present situation in the United States—which certainly might be comparable to the situation in other Western democracies—Buchanan advances the central diagnostic hypothesis that the status quo is not efficient and that the existing legal-constitutional order (or disorder) places everyone in a dilemma in which the privately rational behavior of each person produces a result unsatisfactory to all persons (1977, p. 296).

According to Buchanan's diagnosis, a pragmatic drift of piecemeal adjustments has led into a constitutional dilemma, characterized by an insatiable Leviathan. It is a dilemma from which an escape is possible only through reconstruction of the basic constitutional order and through structural changes conceptually agreed upon by all members in the community (1975, pp. 167, 169).[25]

Although Buchanan's basically contractarian position may perhaps be classified within Hayek's constructivist category, it is to be sharply distinguished from a collectivist-rationalist conception, which obviously is the chief target in Hayek's critique of constructivist rationalism. Hayek's criticism of the collectivist conception—a criticism to which Buchanan explicitly agrees—seems, as Buchanan presumes, to overlook the plausibly acceptable alternative offered by the contractarian position to evolutionism as well as to a collectivist-constructivist rationalism (Buchanan 1977, p. 33).[26] What the contractarian-constructivist conception implies is in fact nothing else than an application of the individualist orientation that is inherent in a libertarian economic perspective to the field of collective decisions.[27] As, with respect to market transactions, the libertarian economist would insist that voluntary exchange indicates agreement among the participants and that agreement among the parties involved is the only criterion on which a trade can be judged to be efficient; the contractarian would insist that, with respect to collective choices, there is also no other criterion for efficiency than voluntary agreement among all participants. If, as one is forced to do within an individualistic framework, one refuses to resort to external criteria for evaluation, in exchange as well as in collective choice, agreement among the participants remains the only internal criterion in both cases (Buchanan 1977, p. 128). Thus, if with respect to the legal-institutional framework, one wants to discriminate without recourse to external evaluation between efficient and inefficient elements, this can be done only on a contractarian basis (Buchanan 1977, p. 127). In doing so, to "say that a situation is inefficient is to say indirectly that there must exist means to move toward efficiency by voluntary agreement" (Buchanan 1977, p. 137).[28] Accordingly, the test to which proposals for reform have to be subjected that is of agreement.[29] Those proposals which are advanced on the basis of the as if contractarian criteria, referred to previously, also are to be subjected to this test. The contractarian conception by no means is a mere cover which may lend pretended legitimacy to any reform for which ones strives, as some critics seem to suspect. The reference to *hypothetical contract* can only be a useful heuristic tool for advancing hypotheses of possible failure and possible improvement. According to the logic of the contractarian approach, the test of these hypotheses lies only in agreement itself.[30] Buchanan points out that beyond agreement there is simply no way for the contractarian to go" (1977, p. 295).

Hayek on Constitutional Reform

If one looks at Hayek's writings, one finds that in spite of his emphasis on evolutionary process and in spite of his deep skepticism about deliberate constructions he in fact does not restrain from rationally criticizing existing political institutions and from advancing proposals for change. On the contrary, notably in his recent writings, he has suggested some quite far-reaching reforms in the basic constitutional structure of the current democratic political systems of the United States.

Thus, with reference to the U.S. experiment in constitutionalism, Hayek comes to the conclusion that measured against historical experience this experiment has to be judged a limited success only or even a failure and that basic constitutional reforms may be inevitable if the United States wants successfuly to realize the aims of the framers of the U.S. Constitution (1960, p. 191; 1979, p. 21).[31] Although that constitution originally was intended effectively to limit governmental power and to secure individual liberty, the current situation, according to Hayek, is characterized by a transformation of the law by inner forces. This transformation will end up with the destruction of individual liberty "if the principles which at present guide that process are allowed to work themselves out to their logical consequences" (1973, pp. 66–67). Very similar to Buchanan's diagnosis of a pragmatic drift, Hayek thesis seems to find the main current threat to the freedom of the individual not in some grand totalitarian design but rather in certain institutional defects within the existing constitutional structure, that is, institutional defects directing the political process toward an impasse and toward a system which nobody wanted (1979, p. xiii; 1973, p. 3). Hayek argues that these are defects of construction of particular institutions in contemporary democratic governments which cause the threatening transformation of a free society into a totalitarian system.[32] According to Hayek, the crucial defect of the predominent model of liberal democratic institutions is that one representative body both lays down the law and directs government, and, thus, the representative assembly is charged with two altogether different tasks[33] which cannot adequately be accomplished by one and the same body (1979, pp. 1, 22).[33]

From his diagnosis Hayek concludes that in the current situation new institutional invention is needed in order to pursue the aims of the founders of liberal constitutionalism (1973, p. 2).[34] To propose basic alterations in the structure of democratic government, Hayek advances a constitutional design which implies that there should be "two distinct representative bodies whereby law-making in the narrow sense as well as government proper would be conducted democratically, but by different, and mutually independent agencies" (1979, pp. 107, xiii).

This is not the place to go into the details of Hayek's proposal.[35] What is of interest with respect to the purpose of this chapter is the question of on which criteria Hayek bases his critical evaluation of the current situation and his proposals for reform. Obviously, the evolutionist conception can offer no criteria here. Hence, one may suspect, as Buchanan does, that Hayek indeed seems to allow for reform through legislation to correct evolutionary aberrations but that he offers no criteria for judgment beyond his own test (1977, p. 37). Although apparently there seem to be no such explicit criteria, a closer look at Hayek's argument shows that—at least implicitly—he in fact refers to a certain criterion, namely, to the very same criterion that is explicitly used in Buchanan's contractarian conception—to *agreement*. Thus he refers to the consent of the people as the ultimate basis on which the legitimacy of constitutional rules rests.[36] Hayek refers to the criterion of agreement in his critical diagnosis of contemporary democratic government when he states that "this machinery produces an aggregate of measures that . . . is not wanted by anybody (1979, p. 6),[37] and when he argues that "if democratic government were really bound to what the masses agree upon there would be little to object to" (1979, p. 99).[38] Finally, he refers to the criterion of agreement when, with respect to his proposals for reform, he suggests that these proposals might be more acceptable to the common opinion of the majority than the existing institutions (Hayek 1977 p. 10).

Thus, one may conclude that when Hayek would make explicit the test to which—according to his opinion—proposals for constitutional change would have to be subjected, he might accept something like a contractarian position as understood by Buchanan. Thus, as was suggested at the beginning of this chapter, after a thorough examination Hayek's evolutionism and Buchanan's contractarianism properly understood are in fact reconcilable and should be reconciled in the interest of a comprehensive and internally consistent *individualistic* conception.

Notes

1. See also Hayek (1960, pp. 34, 36; 1967, p. 72; 1970, p. 9; 1973, p. 18; 1979, pp. 159, 161, 204). For Hayek's discusion of the Scottish moral philosophers as "pre-Darwinian evolutionists in the field of ethics" (Hayek 1967, p. 111), compare, for example, Hayek 1960, p. 57.

2. As Hayek concedes, this certainly does not preclude that deliberate arrangement or organization "for many limited tasks . . . is the most powerful method of effective co-ordination because it enables us to adapt the resulting order much more fully to our wishes" (1973, p. 46).

3. What is concerned here is the conception "of evolution of traditions and habits which made the formation of spontaneous order possible" (Hayek 1967, p. 101).

4. See also Hayek 1960, p. 65; 1967, p. 85; 1973, pp. 8, 28; 1979, pp. 155, 162.

5. Hayek points out that "the evolutionary view is based on the insight that the result of the experimentation of many generations may embody more experience than any one man possesses" (1960, p. 62). See also Hayek 1973, p. 11.

6. Hayek notes, "As we have seen, rules of just conduct did not need to be deliberatly made, though men gradually learned to improve or change them deliberately" (1973, p. 124).

7. Hayek asserts:

the fact that all law arising out of the endeavor to articulate rules of conduct will of necessity possess some desirable properties . . . does not mean that in other respects such law may not develop in very undesirable directions and that when this happens correction by deliberate legislation may not be the only practicable way out. For a variety of reasons the spontaneous process of growth may lead into an impasse from which it will at least not correct quickly enough. . . . It therefore does not mean that we can altogether dispense with legislation (1973, p. 88).

8. According to Hayek "The chief instrument of deliberate change in modern society is legislation. But . . . we are never free to redesign completely the legal system as a whole. . . . Law-making is necessarily a continuous process in which every step produces hitherto unforeseen consequences for what we can or must do next" (1973, p. 65). Hayek asserts, "There is thus certainly room for improvement, but we cannot redesign but only further evolve what we do not fully comprehend" (1979, p. 167). See also Hayek 1967, p. 92; 1969, p. 40; 1970 p. 22.

9. With respect to the conception of spontaneously grown rules Hayek states: "Of course in advanced society only some rules will be of this kind; what we want to emphasize is merely that even such advanced societies will in part owe their order to some such rules" (1973, p. 19).

10. Thus, for example, Hayek points out that the rationalist-constructivist conception "that all institutions which benefit humanity have in the past and ought in the future to be invented in clear awareness of the durable effects that they produce" is opposed to the evolutionist notion "that sometimes grown

institutions which nobody has invented may provide a better framework for cultural growth than more sophisticated designs" (1967, pp. 85, 95). See also Hayek 1973, p. 8.

11. According to Hayek, "The rules governing a spontaneous order must be independent of purpose and be the same, if not necessarily for all members, at least for whole classes of members not individually designated by name. They must ... be rules applicable to an unknown and indeterminable number of persona and instances" (1973, p. 50).

12 Hayek insists, "Strictly speaking, a Constitution ought to consist wholly of organizational rules" (1979, p. 122). A constitution, he points out, "presupposes the existence of a system of rules of just conduct and merely provides a machinery for their regular enforcement" (1979, p. 38). See also Hayek 1973, p. 131: "The distinction between universal rules of just conduct and the rules of organization of government is closely related to, and sometimes explicitly equated to the distinction between private and public law."

13. Hayek asserts that "societies form but states are made" (1979, p. 140).

14. According to Hayek, "To become legitimized, the new rules have to obtain the approval of society at large—not by a formal vote, but by gradually spreading acceptance" (1979, p. 167).

15. Hayek states:

> There is an advantage in obedience to such rules not being coerced ... because it is, in fact, often desirable that rules should be observed only in most instances and that the individual should be able to transgress them ... It is this flexibility of voluntary rules which in the fields of morals makes gradual evolution and spontaneous growth possible, which allows further experience to lead to modification and improvements. Such an evolution is possible only with rules which are neither coercive rules, which can be changed only discontinuously and for all at the same time, rules of this kind allow for gradual and experimental change. The existence of individuals and groups simultaneously observing partially different rules provides the opportunity for the selection of the more effective ones (1960, p. 62).

16. Hayek asserts that "the conception that there must be an unlimited will which is the source of all power is the result of a constructivistic hypostasation" (1979, p. 34). Discussing the conception of popular sovereignty, Hayek states that "its error lies not in the belief that whatever power there is should be in the hands of the people, and that their wishes will have to be expressed by majority decisions, but in the belief that this ultimate source of power must be unlimited" (1979, p. 33). See also Hayek 1977, p. 15.

17. See Hayek 1960, p. 57; 1967, pp. 86, 120; 1973, pp. 1, 10, 21, 1979, pp. 21, 105.

18. The argument that deliberate constructions are built on traditional principles and on experiences of former experiments obviously is very different

from those already mentioned arguments that Hayek uses to explain the difference between an evolutionary conception and a constructivist-rationalist one. Critically reviewing Hayek's evolutionism, Buchanan states, "The American cannot, and should not , neglect the fact that his own heritage of freedom although owing much to its European antecedents, was deliberately constructed in large part by James Madison and his compatriots. Theirs were no invisible hand" (1977, p. 39).

19. Hayek explains:

> I have so far carefully avoided saying that evolution is identical with progress, but when it becomes clear that it was the evolution of a tradition which made civilization possible, we may at least say that spontaneous evolution is necessary if not a sufficient condition of progress. And though it clearly produces also much that we did not foresee and do not like when we see it, it does bring to ever-increasing numbers what they have been mainly striving for (1979, p. 168).

20. According to Buchanan, "Institutions evolve, but those that survive and prosper need not be those which are best as evaluated by the men who live under them. Institutional evolution may place man increasingly in situations described by the dilemma made familiar in modern game theory" (1975, p. x). See also Buchanan 1977, p. 31: "The forces of social evolution alone contain within their workings no guarantee that socially efficient results will emerge over time."

21. In commenting on his criticism of Hayek's position Buchanan states: "My criticism is based on what I interpret to be the basic thrust of Hayek's argument. . . . In particular places, Hayek seems to concede many if not all of the points that may be advanced in opposition. My purpose here is not one of exegesis, but is instead that of offering hopefully constructive criticism" (1977, p. 30n.).

22. With reference to the affinity that R. Nozick's approach in "Anarchy, State, and Utopia" (1974) shows to Hayek's conception, Bucanan states: "Both Hayek and Nozick may be classified broadly as evolutionists in their positive explanation of how the law emerges. They go further, however, and make normative inferences to the effect that explicit efforts toward constructive reforms are not desired" (1977, p. 293). See also Buchanan 1977, p. 125; 1975, p. 194.

23. Buchanan asserts, "But something akin to a contractarian position seems to be essential if we are to go beyond explanation, if we are to be able to evaluate existing elements of the constitutional order with any prospect of securing improvement" (1977, p. 293).

24. With reference to Hayek's interpretations of law as the outcome of an evolutionary process Buchanan states, "In historical fact, evolutionary elements may explain much of the emergence and development of law. Acceptance of this however, does not negate the application of contractual constructivist criteria

in an evaluation of that law which exists, and which might be willfully modified" (1975, p. 183).

25. Buchanan explains that "this scenario ... is not the working out of some grand design. ... [It] is explainable as the unintended consequence of individual actions, taken pragmatically, locally, and with no sense of overall design or purpose, either destructive or constructive" (1977, p. 297).

26. According to Buchanan, "Hayek is so distrustful of man's explicit attempts at reforming institutions that he accepts uncritically the evolutionary alternative. We may share much of Hayek's skepticism about social and institutional reform, however, without elevating the evolutionary process to an ideal role" (1975, p. 194).

27. As Buchanan states, the libertarian and the contractarian not only share the individualist value premise, in addition "their diagnoses of current social malaise are likely to be similar in dondemning overextended governmental authority" (1977, p. 23).

28. Buchanan points out that the "definition of an existing set of institutions as nonoptimal in the sense that it does not reflect consensus means strictly that changes are possible on which *all* members of the group may agree" (1962, p. 319).

29. According to Buchanan, "the appropriate criterion for goodness is to be found in the process of agreement on potential change. ... A change is defined to be good because it is agreed to by the members of the community" (1979, p. 352).

30. See Buchanan 1977, pp. 139-140.

31. Hayek asserts that the "framers of the American Constitution articulated the conception of a limiting constitution. ... Their chief aim was to provide institutional safeguards of individual freedom; and the device in which they placed their faith was the separation of powers. In the form in which we know this division of powers between legislature, the judiciary, and the administration, it has not achieved what it was meant to achieve. ... The first attempt to secure individual liberty by constitutions has evidently failed" (1973, p. 1). See also Hayek 1979, p. 105.

32. Hayek finds that this "threatening development towards a totalitarian state is made inevitable by certain deeply entrenched defects of construction of the generally accepted type of democratic government" (1979, p. xiii).

33. According to Hayek, "The ideal of a democratic control of government and that of the limitation of government by law are thus different ideals that certainly cannot be accomplished by placing into the same representative body both rule-making and governmental powers" (1979, p. 26).

34. Hayek asks, "What can we do today, in the light of the experience gained, to accomplish the aims which, nearly two hundred years ago, the father of the Constitution of the United States of America for the first time attempted to secure by deliberate construction?" (1979, p. 105).

35. With respect to the difference between rules of just conduct and constitutional rules and, hence, between legislation proper and constitution making, Hayek specifies his proposal in that "a three-tiered system of representative bodies is needed, of which one should be concerned with the semi-permanent framework of the constitution. . . . , another with the continuous task of gradual improvement of the general rules of just conduct, and a third with the current conduct of government" (1979, pp. 9, 38, 122).

36. Hayek asserts that the "legitimacy rested in the last resort on the approval by the people at large of certain fundamental principles underlying and limiting all government" (1979, p. 35). See also Hayek 1979, pp, 3, 4, 6, 17, 33, 34; 1960, pp. 160, 180).

37. According to Hayek, The "activities of modern government produce aggregate results that few people have either wanted or foreseen. . . . [The] particular set of institutions . . . has produced many results which nobody likes" (1979, p. 1). See also Hayek 1979, p. 4).

38. That Hayek, however, will not entirely rely on agreement as the criterion of goodness is indicated, for example, by his statement that "the agreement among many people on the justice of a particular rule may indeed be a good though not an infalliable test of its justice" (1979, p. 7). Compare this with Buchanan's statement that "that rule is acceptable which is itself defined by agreement among all participants in the game. We may, if desired, substitute fair for acceptable here, and if we want to go one step further semantically, we may replace fair with just. . . . Note carefully that the attribute assigned to the rule in this way is derived from the agreement instead of any independent quality or property of the rule itself" (1977, p. 294).

References

Buchanan, James M. 1962. "Marginal Notes on Reading Political Philosophy." In *The Calculus of Consent–Logical Foundations of Constitutional Democracy,* by James M. Buchanan and G. Tullock, p. 307. Ann Arbor: University of Michigan Press.

––––––. 1975. *The Limits of Liberty–between Anarchy and Leviathan.* Chicago: University of Chicago Press.

––––––. 1978. *Freedom of Constitutional Contract, Perspectives of a Political Economist.* College Station: Texas A&M University Press.

––––––. 1979. "Constitutional Constraints on Governmental Taxing Power." In *Ordo* 30 (Stuttgart and New York): 349-359.

Hayek, F.A. von. *1961. The Constitution of Liberty.* Chicago: University of Chicago Press.

––––––. 1967. *Studies in Philosophy, Politics and Economics.* London: Routledge and Kegan Paul.

———. 1969. *Freiburger Studien–Gesammelte Aufsätze.* Tubingen: J.C.B. Mohr.

———. 1970. *Die Irrtümer des Konstruktivismus.* Salzburg.

———. 1973. *Rules and Order.* Law, Legislation, and Liberty, vol. 1. Chicago: University of Chicago Press.

———. 1977. *Drei Vorlesungen über Demokratie, Gerechtigkeit und Sozialismus.* Tubingen: J.C.B. Mohr.

———. 1979. *The Political Order of a Free People.* Law, Legislation and Liberty, vol. 3. Chicago: University of Chicago Press.

7 The Muddle of the Middle

F. A. von Hayek

When thirty-six years ago I inscribed *The Road to Serfdom* to the Socialists of all parties, I am afraid this was not least aimed at an influential wing of the Conservative party. Indeed, I quoted in it an observation made a few years earlier by the late Harold Nicolson, then a National Labour M.P., to the effect that in the House of Commons among the back-benchers of the Conservative party the most gifted were all socialists at heart. Among the most recent experiences that have impressed upon me the all-pervasive nature of socialist views is a book with the significant title, *The Middle Way,* which has probably much influenced the thinking of many of the present generation of Conservatives.

In the 1930s this book was the significant symbol of a growing trend which had appeared forty years earlier. It commenced among the liberals, and it happened even before the beginning of this century that a liberal chancellor of the exchequer coined the famous phrase, we are all socialists now. This trend was the cause of the decline of Britain's economy and of Britain's general standing in the world and led to the erosion of the tradition of freedom that had made her great and even of most of what had been distinctive British traditions. These traditions that had enabled Britain to pull so far ahead of the rest of the civilized world did not begin so very much earlier. The great historian F.W. Maitland pointed out that "in the sixteenth and early seventeenth century the political structure of England was not yet fundamentally different from that of the continental countries and it might still have seemed uncertain whether she would develop a highly centralized absolute monarchy as did the countries on the continent." What made England distinct was the civil war and the glorious revolution which for two hundred years effectively curtailed the powers of government.

The reaction against this began during the last quarter of the nineteenth century, largely under continental influence. It operated most strongly among the intellectually most active, most well meaning, and most progressive. The only large section of the population among whom socialism in this country ever conquered a clear majority was that of the intellectuals. The infiltration of socialism into the Liberal party, of course, was greatest and assumed an extent which deprived it of the right to call itself *liberal.* However, the genius for compromise and the realistic sense of the Conservative party for what is politically possible has had a similar effect on it. I am not speaking without sympathy. In the gift for muddling through—it used to be called *fortwursteln*—my native Austria was the only country which can rival, and perhaps even has surpassed,

England. This may be the source of a certain instinctive sympathy between the inhabitants of the two countries. However, this contempt for principle leads to catastrophe, at least when it leads to the attempt to reconcile irreconcilable doctrines. One cannot create harmony out of conflicting principles, and socialism is not half right but all wrong. It must be resisted in principle if one is not to be dragged step by step into a system which is both totalitarian and ineffective. The Conservative party has failed in this because it refused to be bound by principles but abandoned principles in the service of expediency.

The title of this chapter was chosen many months ago, and most of it was written before I saw Sir Ian Gilmour's Cambridge lecture which asserts so much of what I shall be arguing against (and I have only a day or two ago encountered his book *Inside Right*). Since he has chosen me as the representative of what he regards as a doctrinaire approach, I can hardly avoid saying a few words about his advocacy of what he calls a free and mixed economy, which is, of course, a circumlocution for an economy which is partly free and partly not. Indeed his lecture was essentially devoted, after some well deserved praise for Mrs. Thatcher, to restoring discussion of fundamental principles at the heart of political debate and showing that she actually believed in something and to arguing that conservatives should at most "hold a theory which is not ideological and which distrusts abstract thought." Because conservatism is not a system but judges issues on their merits and not by doctrine, it is capable of appealing to socialist instincts when this seems expedient. No wonder that Eric Heffer explained in *The Times* that he would find it easier to get on with the heirs of Macmillan and R. Butler than with people like Mrs. Thatcher and Sir Keith Joseph who "fanatically believe in what they are doing." Fortunately, they understand that compromising with socialism can lead only into more and more socialism even if for a time it may help at elections.

The crucial difference between a statesman and a mere politician is that the former does not concede particular measures to gain a few votes but undertakes to show people what benefits them by sticking to the principles he has professed. If he is convinced that only the restoration of the market economy can gain for the masses what they yearn for and if he has gained an election by professing that principle, he must cease angling for the votes of particular groups by offering them special advantages.

Gilmour can be a little unfair when it suits his argument. To illustrate, immediately after he referred to me as a threat to reform, he pointed at the warning example of President Cleveland's saying in 1887 that it would be against principles to aid victims of repeated harvest failure. Of course, in a wealthy country there is a strong case for government providing *outside the market* a minimum for those poorest victims of acts of God or the king's enemies who are unable to provide for themselves. But this has nothing to do with a redistribution of incomes according to some nonexisting principles of social justice, or even with creating of jobs for particular people which will give them the income they believe that they deserve.

This misrepresentation is probably due to Gilmour's having read only *The Road to Serfdom* but not, as I believe Mrs. Thatcher did, also *The Constitution of Liberty*. Gilmour might have discovered there that I do not reject all aspects of the welfare state, which his wing of the Conservative party is so proud of having created, but regard it as a frightful muddle which badly needs sorting out—a typical result of following expediency and disregarding principle.

I do not wish to be led too far away from my original plan by commenting on Gilmour's apology for muddling through. But since he, like so many other conservatives, likes to appeal to Edmund Burke, one might take the opportunity of reminding him that Edmund Burke, like David Hume and Lord Halifax, to whom he also appeals, were Whigs and not Tories. I strongly feel that if I could talk to Edmund Burke I would find him, as Adam Smith did, "the only person he ever knew who thought on economic subjects exactly as he did without any personal communication having passed between them" Would Gilmour agree with Burke's opinion "against an overdoing of any sort of administration, and more especially the most momentous of all, meddling on the party of authority: the meddling with the sustenance of the people"?

It is ultimately not humility but the same arrogance of omniscience which socialism shows if conservatives believe that they can dispense with principles and claim to be able to judge each case on its individual merits or that, as Gilmour puts it, "political theory should never get in the way of sensible political action." If sensible political action in this particular case means what brings most votes by handing out special benefits to particular groups, this is, of course, the way in which the present collossus of government has been built up, and it becomes merely a matter of taste as to which particular groups ought to be specially benefitted.

The heart of the matter and the source of the intellectual confusion, which has much more than any moral differences, particularly in this country, converted both the left and the right to socialist conceptions of the tasks of government, must now be considered. There is no better way to analyze the intellectual sources of the acceptance of redistribution as a goal of policy than to examine the argument of John Stuart Mill in his *Principles of Political Economy*—the influence of which is shown by the fact that in some parts of the world it was still used as a college text a full hundred years after its publication in 1848. No doubt Mill was not the only one whose thought moved that way—after all, Karl Marx also started from the same Ricardian base—but he was a most influential man whose reputation as a defender of intellectual liberty made it easier for him to smuggle socialist ideas into economics. In his case it is also particularly easy to show how false economics led him to his conclusions. Indeed, his explicit statements, though explainable by his intellectual background, are really of almost unbelievable intellectual naiveté and reveal a complete incomprehension of the central problem of economic theory, namely, what determines which things are produced and how. "The laws and conditions of the production of wealth," he argued, "partake of the character of physical truth. . . . It is not so with the Distribution of Wealth. That is a matter of human institutions only. *The things once there* [!] Mankind, individually and collectively, can do with them as they like. They can place them at the disposal of whoever they please and on whatever terms" (P.O.P.E., II, 1, § 1). To rub it in he repeats later, "Of the two great departments of Political Economy, the production of wealth and its distribution, the consideration of values has to do with the latter only" (Ibid. III, 1, § 1). Thus, people would know what, how, and how much of each thing to produce without market prices telling them. Before considering further this amazing assertion that one can explain production without examining what determines its direction and method, a word should be said about where this inevitably led Mill. If the product became available irrespective of the guiding factor of prices which told the individuals what to do, including the manner of the division and coordination of labor, of course, it would become a matter of arbitrary will of the owners of the given product which just was there to decide to whom it ought to go. This raised the problem not of how the shares contributed by the different participants of the process were determined but of how human will should distribute the total. This then became a moral problem which still left open whose moral duty it was to arrange the distribution. As Mill seems to have been vaguely aware that the classical conception of distributive justice, like all moral rules, applied only to the actions of persons to whom established moral rules assigned control over particular assets, he apparently invented and at any rate gave currency to the new conception of social justice, implying that society (he was typically afraid of frankly saying *government*) ought to decide how these resources ought to be shared.

One does not know what Mill would have said if he had recognized that this wealth was available only because of the different remunerations offered to people with unavoidably different gifts and opportunities. How would he tell them to fit their efforts (and the use of the resources under their control) into a complex pattern which nobody could survey or determine in all its essential detail? The fact is that this order just would not be there except for a system of differential offers that has nothing to do with justice and cannot be determined by considerations of justice. What could justice mean in an order in which each person's merits could be judged only in the light of circumstances that that person alone could know and in which it was necessary for the achievement of merits that each adjust his activities to that particular fraction of all known facts which only he could know? What could justice mean where the apparent command of wealth was not based on what others thought a person deserved or ought to do but on what a process of evolution of society that nobody directed or could have directed had placed within the reach of each? Thus, one could use most distinct opportunities, small or large, for his advantage only because others, unknown to him, knew of other facts, equally unknown to him, which made his activities valuable to them.

John Stuart Mill was the saint of rationalism for a good reason. Mill's ideas are the roots of the self-destructive character of a rationalist or constructivistic view of how civilization could be organized. Since Mill, this muddle about facts has guided policy and most of the strivings of people of good will, who were inspired by a false picture, based on a worldwide division of labor, of how a society worked. It was from Mill's muddle (and the similar deceptions of Marx) and from the confusion of those pretended defenders of liberty who proclaimed a new moral postulate which required a complete suppression of individual freedom that the whole muddle of the middle derived. The ideal of freedom was increasingly relegated to second place by the idea of social justice. However, the two are incompatible. If one accepts the principle of social justice, one cannot preserve the market economy which provides that which social justice would like to distribute. The two principles are antagonistic and irreconcilable. There can be no halfway house between them. As the promise of social justice cannot be generally satisfied and also cannot be refused to all others once it has been conceded to some, there can be no question about where one's choice must lie if one really wants to help the poor.

The social product which is now maintaining a human population of this world four or five hundred times as large as that which man could achieve in the natural hunting and gathering stage is owed only to the division of labor, skills, and knowledge. This division could never have been designed or planned, but it arose through and is now maintained by the guiding service of competitive market prices and wages that tell each person where its efforts can make the largest contribution to the total. These self-generating signals, which inform the individuals about the combined effects of thousands of events of which they can have no direct information, bring about an adaptation of the individual efforts to the unknown. No central direction could achieve this adaptation because the knowledge of all the facts of which the market takes account is spread among thousands and cannot be known to any central authority. It is, of course, impossible to improve signals when one does not know what determines them. Wealth, which social justice would like to distribute as a reward for merit and need, is, therefore, due to the circumstance that the direction of individual efforts is guided by a choice between returns which depends largely on accidental circumstances of time and place and is effected but not conclusively determined by what the individual can know or do. Thus, the wealth which the advocates of social justice want to redistribute would not exist if social justice reigned. Social justice is a fraud, a promise to distribute what one would not have if one followed its bidding. Wealth just would not be there or would rapidly disappear if the ordering by the principles of the market that now guide its production were replaced by some others which would give to each that to which he imagines himself to be entitled. Social justice is about the worst product of democratic demagoguery which has yet emerged.

This is the basic reason why there can be no stable halfway house between a market economy and socialism and why if one gives a finger to the socialists they will be able to take the whole hand. Once one has granted privileges on the grounds of social justice, there is no stopping place which can be politically defended. A democracy will at best be able to confine privileges to a majority and deny them to a minority. The middle way is sheer confusion. It is the typical compromise of the politician who lacks a moral philosophy (which he contemptuously calls an ideology) and becuase of this lack is led to a policy of muddling through and accepting the facts of life.

By its acceptance the Conservative party bears a great part of the responsibility for the decline of Britain. This period of decline was governed by what is called *Butskelism*. I knew Mr. H. Gaitskell as a university assistant whom I induced to go to Vienna in the hope that he would learn some better economics—while I, unfortunately, had no such opportunity with the not much older Mr. R.A. Butler with whom I might have been more successful. On all crucial issues of the present time there is no prospect of the Conservative party's successfully using this last opportunity of pulling Britain out of the mire unless it dissociates itself thoroughly from this unfortunate period of its history.

To return to the imminent problems of the present time, it is necessary to consider what is now referred to as *monetarism*. This is, of course, no more than a new-fangled name for the good old quantity theory of money. There is no doubt whatever that inflation can be stopped at any time and can be stopped only by cutting down increases in the quantity of money. What I said nearly forty years ago in the very first lecture I was ever allowed to give in England appears to me as true as ever. It would be one of the worst things which could ever befall us (but which John Maynard Keynes has unfortunately achieved) if the general public should ever again cease to believe in the elementary propositions of the quantity theory. Admittedly in its classic form, as now revived by Milton Friedman, it grossly oversimplifies things by making it all an issue of statistical aggregates and averages. First, unfortunately the quantity of money is not a measurable homogenous magnitude but consists of a wide range of mutually more or less substitutable things of varying degrees of liquidity. Second, its value depends not simply on the total quantity of it being available but also on the variable demand for it. Third, the harmful effects of an excessive supply of money consist not merely in changes of the average price level but quite as much in the distortion of the whole structure of relative prices and the consequent misdirection of productive efforts which it causes.

Nevertheless, there is no doubt whatever that inflation is caused solely by an undue increase in the quantity of money and that it can and must be prevented under the prevailing arrangements only by the restriction of the basic money supplied by the central bank. There is no such thing as a cost-push inflation, and all inflation is brought about by what that agency of government is made to do. Nobody else can do anything about it. The chief practical issue today is how fast inflation can be and ought to be stopped. On this issue my difference from Friedman makes me take an even more radical position. The artificial stimulus which inflation gives to business and employment lasts only so long as inflation accelerates, that is, so long as prices turn out to be higher than expected. Inflation clearly cannot accelerate indefinitely. But as soon as it ceases to accelerate, all the windfalls due to prices turning out higher than expected which kept unprofitable businesses and employments going disappear. Every slowing down of inflation, therefore, must produce temporary conditions of extensive failures and unemployment. No inflation has yet been terminated without a stabilization crisis. To advocate that inflation should be slowed down gradually over a period of years is to advocate a long period of protracted misery. No government could stand such a course.

If inflation is to be stopped, it must be done here and now. After World War I the United States brought prices down by one-third in six months (August 1920 to February 1921). The suffering was great, but six months later a new boom was under way. There is no question now of actually bringing prices down but merely of stopping any further rise. If this is not done by a determined government like the present, it will not be done before the pound finally collapses entirely after a vain attempt to conceal inflation by price controls (called an *incomes policy*).

The practical difficulties are due, of course, to the fact that because of the alleged beneficial effect on employment, the country has been lured into the practice of increasing the financing of government expenditure by borrowing. At the moment Britain just does not know how to maintain the existing apparatus of government without continuing to inflate. I do not want to discuss here these financial difficulties about which, frankly, I do not know enough. On questions of political possibility, even if I had the opportunity, which I have not, I would never presume to advise Mrs. Thatcher. My concern is solely with the political philosophy which must guide Britain if the country is to get out of the vicious circle of decline which the socialistic tendencies of past conservative policy have helped to bring about. If I have any hesitation it is whether it was not over-confident or excessively brave to begin with a reduction of taxation before expenditure had been cut. But that touches on those political issues on which I am not competent to advise.

The remainder of this chapter will be devoted to the crucial relations among monetary policy, trade unions, and unemployment. All the emphasis on monetary policy as a means of curing unemployment was, of course, an attempt at seeking a way out from the consequences or drawing attention from the consequences of the labor monopolies which Britain had allowed to develop. All Britain's troubles, including Lord Keynes's false proposals for a cure, are due to the attempts to evade the real issue, that is, that a market economy cannot function if wages are not determined by competition but by political power. All Keynesianism had its origin in a desperate but vain attempt to cope with the result of the rigidity of wages at a time when a mistaken attempt at restoring the gold standard at the old parity would have made necessary an actual reduction of all wages. This attempt to maintain employment by adapting the general level of prices to politically determined wages has failed and was bound to fail. It has only increased the effects of monopolistically determined wages on employment and made the solution infinitely more difficult than it would have been fifty odd years ago There is still no other way out than that which ought to have been chosen then.

The conception that there is some simple correlation between the volume of aggregate demand for final goods and the total volume of employment derives from the experience of the shopkeeper that a strong demand for his goods secures his prosperity. The conception of such a relation as exists between the strength with which one may suck at one end of a pipe and the pull of the suction at the other end is of course the crudest possible misrepresentation that has been periodically reintroduced into scientific discussion, most recently and with devastating effect by Lord Keynes. The incredible crudity of this approach, congenial to the minds for whom scientific method exhausts itself in measuring the connection between changes of two observable magnitudes, ought to have been exposed long ago. The volume of employment is not determined by the relation of total demand to the total supply of goods and services but by the correspondence or noncorrespondence between the distribution of demand among the different goods and services and the proportions in which these different things are offered. This applies not only to the horizontal or cross-sectional but equally to the longitudinal or vertical distribution within the stream of goods and services providing for future needs: the degree to which the volume of this stream is filled up or reduced and the corresponding shifts of demand from later to earlier stages of production or vice versa. Both these correspondence can be brought about only by appropriate changes in relative prices of the different means of production and a prompt adaptation of the quantities supplied to quantities demanded. Demand for labor is not a homogenous aggregate but an extremely diversified force with complex interactions among the parts, which defy any helpful summarization by statistics. All that is certain is that any rigidity of wages and any refusal to adjust them promptly to changing conditions must make it impossible for particular workers to find employment at the given wages, which is a condition that by various interconnections is bound to spread. Freezing the relations among the wages of different kinds of labor must produce unemployment.

The second elementary proposition which is currently overlooked is that particular wages raised above the market level by trade-union monopoly will actually attract capital to the industry protected by a labor monopoly against the competition from lower paid workers. This capital then displaces some workers and deprives them as well as workers elsewhere of the means of increasing their productivity. The reduced number of workers that can be employed at the higher wages are equipped with more capital per head at the expense of other workers. It is not the general scarcity of capital which determines the achievable productivity but the artificial scarcity of a particular kind of worker which determines how many of them it is advantageous to replace by machinery. At the expense of the rest, a restricted number of workers may indeed claim an undue share of the total capital supply and deprive less well-equipped workers of their more urgent need for such assistance. In such instances, the personnel of a whole industry may become a privileged elite as the contrived shortage of labor causes an above-average return both to labor and the capital (newly) employed in it. Although such a rise in wages may well take some income from the old stockholders, it will not reduce that of new investors or of those who actually run the industry. Moreover, it will hold down the wages of workers elsewhere whose productivity would have been increased more substantially if the capital went where it would go in a free market. A trade-union demand, thus, may not be in excess of the employers' capacity to pay but may be very harmful to other workers.

Except for the remaining fools who still believe that capital can be effectively increased by simply increasing the quantity of money, it should be obvious to anybody today that the gain of the best organized workers is the loss of the rest. To make rationalization necessary by driving up wages is not a triumph of but a loss for the working class. It means robbing the poorer but less well organized to benefit the much better off and at the same time obtaining a smaller total product.

Until it becomes generally understood that the chief sufferers from trade-union monopolies are the workers in other industries—and not merely those who are prevented from getting better jobs or any job at all but also those who earn less in their jobs than they would if the available capital was no deflected to those in whom the labor monopoly is strongest—the problem of employment will not be solved. It is one of the intellectual absurdities of the present time that capitalism is blamed for unemployment. It is not the market economy but the inhibition of the market process by organized power—chiefly the trade unions but also the monopoly of the issue of money—which prevents competition from clearing the market. The damage which has been done by the dominating belief that the market is unable to find use for all possible contributions to human needs is incalculable. The damage done by the exclusive power of government in supplying us with a single kind of money which must be used whether it is good or bad will not be discussed here. The time has not yet come when this can be changed, though it will come. No monetary policy can undo the damage done by inappropriately high wages. The available capital is distributed in such a way the productivity of a section of the workers is greatly raised but the others are left out in the cold.

The other great privileged monopoly and the chief cause of the present troubles is the trade union. This is not to suggest that trade unions ought to be suppressed. But they must be wholly and radically deprived of all the special privileges which legislation and jurisdiction, foolishly and recklessly, have conferred upon them. It is on this issue that there exists a fundamental division within the Conservative party between those who really believe in the market economy and those who still think that by appropriate intervention and control it is possible in fact and politically even desirable to correct the market by a little judicious intervention in the direction of social justice. The hope that the new barons, as they have been correctly called, can be persuaded by friendly talks to renounce the privileges on which their arbitrary powers rest must prove an illusion. An appeal over their heads must be made to the rank and file of the working people of this country who are already showing that they are much more responsible than their leaders.

It does not appear to have really entered general consciousness how completely anomalous and contrary to all the basic principles of law which have made Britain great and how destructive of her wealth are those privileges which legislation has conferred upon trade unions. This was done chiefly by the liberals in 1906 who, as Robert Moss points out in *The Collapse of Democracy,* "passed a bill drawn up by the first generation of Labour MPs in keeping of an electoral promise [and] quite literally had no idea of what they were doing."

The following are a few samples of the response which this action provoked at the time among English jurisprudents and foreign observers:

The Trade Dispute Act of 1906 conferred upon trade unions a freedom from civil liability for the commission of even the most heinous wrong by the union or its servants, and in short conferred upon every trade union a privilege and protection from not possessed by any other person or body of persons whether corporate or incorporated ... [It] makes the trade union a privileged body exempted from the ordinary law of the land. No such privileged body has ever before been created by an English Parliament. ... It stimulated among workmen the fatal illusion that workmen could aim at the attainment, not of equity, but of privilege (A.V. Dicey 1914, pp. 14–17).

The Trade Dispute Act of 1906 conferred upon the unions an immunity from prosecution on the ground of acts of their agents; the immunity stands in flagrant disagreement with the law of agency and the law as to companies represented by their officers in accordance with the statutory power order of 1883. The reason for this discordant state of the law is to be found in the resolve of legislation to secure for the unions a favourable position in their struggle with the employers (Vinogradoff 1925, p. 10).

In short, it put trade unionism in the same privileged position which the Crown enjoyed until ten years ago in respect to wrongful acts committed on its behalf (MacDermot 1957, p. 147).

It is difficult, at the present time, to realize how this measure must have struck people who still believed in a state and a legal system that centered in the institution of private property. For in relaxing the law of conspiracy in respect to peaceful picketing—which practically amounted to legalization of trade union action implying the threat of force—and in exempting trade union funds from liability in action *for torts,* which practically amounted to enacting that trade unions could do no wrong—this measure in fact resigned to the trade unions part of the authority of the state and granted to them a position of privilege which the formal extension of the exemption to employers' unions was powerless to affect (Josef Schumpeter 1942, p. 321).

During the last month, there has been a long correspondence on legislation and the rule of law in *The Times.* Nobody has pointed out that legislation can destroy and has destroyed the rule of law. Although it is heartening to find a British judge trying to restore it, it is probably true that Parliament has already decided otherwise. However, the rule of law and special privilege are irreconcilable. No everything which an almighty Parliament lays down is a rule of justice.

It is fortunate that recent developments have given this country a new constitutional tool by which the established power of politically organized groups can be broken. The entry into the European community was achieved by a referendum. At a time when the most crucial issue for the future of Britain is the abolition of the privileges on which the power of those rest who today chiefly determine who is to represent labor in Parliament, this opens a way for a direct appeal to the people which may prove the only escape from a fatal dilemma. There is little doubt about what the answer of the great majority of the British people would be to the single question of whether the trade unions should be deprived of all the special privileges conceded to them and be placed under the same law that everybody else has to obey. Unless the new barons are deprived of the powers they have thoughtlessly been granted, they will always be forced to abuse them. No representatives of special interests can be allowed to have compulsory powers.

This is a matter of decisive importance for the future of this country which must be settled. The battle for the survival of Britain as a wealthy people of consideration among the advanced nations is now being fought within the Conservative party. Conservatism must not mean that the party must persist in past mistakes. The socialist theories of the thirties were an attempt to reconcile irreconcilables. They must be abandoned, or British freedom and prosperity are lost. There is still hope that Britain can be saved from becoming the historical showpiece of a society which destroyed itself by dedicating itself to social purposes.

References

Dicey, A.V. 1914. *Law and Opinion.* 2d ed. London: MacMillan.

Gilmour, Ian. 1977. *Inside Right,* p. 294. London: Hutchinson.

MacDermot. 1957. *Protections from Power under English Law.* London.

Moss, Robert. 1976. *The Collapse of Democracy,* p. 300. New Rochelle, N.Y.: Arlington House.

Schumpeter, Josef. 1942. *Capitalism, Socialism and Democracy.* New York: Harper & Row.

Vinogradoff, Paul. 1925. *Custom and Right.* Oslo.

Codetermination in the West: The Case of Germany

Svetozar Pejovich

In recent years, most West European countries have joined Germany in actively promoting labor participation in the management of business enterprises. Codetermination, as this development has come to be called, is a major post-war social experiment in Western Europe. As in Germany—the undisputed leader in the use of codetermination schemes—labor participation in the management of business firms is being introduced into the social life of West European countries. The major feature of codetermination in Western Europe is that it is mandated by law. This study shows that codetermination laws attenuate the right of ownership and contractual freedom and, consequently, represent a major weakening of capitalism in the West. The laws on codetermination are in effect a major vehicle through which socialism has been creeping into Western societies.

Codetermination laws differ from one country to another. However, they all have a common denominator: labor participation in the management of business firms. Labor is represented on the board of directors and is given an active role in decision-making. Where the governing authority of firms is divided into two tiers, as in Germany and the Netherlands, the labor representatives sit on the supervisory board.[1] Where there is a single board of directors, the employees' representatives take their place in that body. Labor unions have been "bribed" into supporting the codetermination movement by having been given either the right to appoint their own representatives on the board of directors, or the assurance that they will be able to control the worker representatives, or both.

Two major explanations for the introduction of codetermination in Western Europe are the enhancement of industrial democracy and the reduction of worker alienation. The former president of France, M. Giscard d'Estaing, said "participation of workers' representatives in the life of their company reflects the workers' aspirations not to be left out of decisions that concern them."[2] The former Chancellor of Germany, Willy Brandt, stated in 1973 that he considered the development of company laws in the meaning of codetermination by employees and workers to be one of the main tasks during this legislative period. Just as agreement was found with respect to the Shop Constitution Law,

---

This chapter was originally presented at the University of Cologne in January, 1982, and reprinted from the Heritage Lecture Series #10.

a mutual solution will be found here too by starting from the principle of equal rights and even balance of weight of employees and employers.[3]

The European Commission has proclaimed labor participation in the management of business firms as a fundamental objective of the community.

> The increasing recognition is being given to the democratic imperative that those who will be substantially affected by decisions made by social and political institutions must be involved in the making of those decisions. Employees not only derive their income from enterprises which employ them, but they devote a large portion of their daily lives to the enterprise. Decisions taken by or in the enterprise can have a substantial effect on their economic circumstances, both immediately and in the longer term; the satisfaction which they derive from their work; their health and physical condition; the time and energy which they can devote to their families and to activities other than work; and even their sense of dignity and autonomy as human beings.[4]

Implicit in the discussion of the codetermination movement is the conviction shown by European intellectuals that labor participation is desirable and that the real problem is one of developing the appropriate legal framework. Since the merits of codetermination are decided at the outset, no effort is made to determine the cost of this social reform.

Codetermination has also reached across the Atlantic Ocean and has established a foothold in the United States. The election of Douglas Fraser, President of the United Auto Workers, as a director of the Chrysler Corporation, is best known but not the only example of codetermination in the United States. It has, however, focused attention on codetermination in the country. Peter Drucker said:

> It seems apparent that codetermination, even when it is merely debated and then set aside, is an explosive issue that has important political as well as social ramifications. We in this country would do well to pay greater attention to this issue.[5]

A few early examples of codetermination in the United States have created the misleading impression that, unlike in Europe, labor participation in this country will develop contractually. In most cases, including the Chrysler Corporation, directors were elected by the stockholders and serve at their pleasure.

The California Labor Relations Act (CALRA) has in effect mandated codetermination in the agri-business in California. However, codetermination in Western Europe and codetermination introduced by CALRA are substantially different. In Europe, labor representatives on the boards of directors participate jointly with other directors in the decision-making process at the corporate level. Under CALRA a significant amount of decision-making power is simply transferred to labor unions. We shall discuss CALRA in more detail later in this study.

So, codetermination means the participation of the employees as well as labor unions in the firm's decision-making process. Codetermination laws grant workers and labor unions an important property right: to participate directly in managerial decisions including investment plans and the allocation of earnings. As Armen Alchian said:

> The proposal for [codetermination] is simply a proposal to transfer wealth of stockholders to employees, or more accurately to transfer a share of the stockholders' specific asset wealth to the providers of generalized, non-specific resources—called the employees. And it has no other viable economic function. That is why it does not appear voluntarily.[6]

Whatever the facade of words, the major objective of codetermination is a transfer of wealth from the stockholders to the employees. This redistribution of wealth has social and economic consequences which arise from the interference by codetermination with the essential characteristics of a private property capitalist economy: *the capitalization into the present market-value of foreseeable future consequences of current decisions.* This interference with the working of capitalism stems from changes in the prevailing relationship among shareholders; managers, employees, and labor unions; incentive structures; and the strength of the link between decision-making and who actually bears the cost or reward from changes in the market value of assets. In general, codetermination cannot be regarded as an unimportant experiment. It has the potential for bringing about profound changes in the quality of social life. Since Germany has been the undisputed leader in the development of codetermination in the West, this study will concentrate on the development of codetermination in that country.

Philosophical Foundations

The idea of labor participation in the management of business firms has a long tradition in Germany. References to labor participation can be traced back to the early 1800s.

As with most social programs, the codetermination movement in the West is the consequence of a set of ideas. Similarly, codetermination is not in practice an exact replica of the ideas from which it was born, but to understand the development of codetermination it is then necessary briefly to discuss its philosophical foundations.

German conservative Catholic philosophy and Marxism have made major contributions to the birth of codetermination. Those two philosophical movements have only one common trait: a strong anti-capitalist bias. What were the objections to capitalism which eventually gave rise to the idea of codetermination?

The capitalist system rests on the right of private ownership and contractual freedom. These two institutions supply incentives that generate specific and predictable behaviors. The pattern of behavior that stems from the basic institutions of capitalism is consistent with both economic efficiency and individual liberty. The survival trait for the individual in a capitalist society is to seek and negotiate voluntary exchange. The behavior of the individual is guided by the principles of self-interest, self-responsibility, and self-determination. "Methodological individualism" is the term that is used to define the position of the individual in a free society.

Methodological individualism does not mean that capitalism rejects tradition and morality. Tradition and moral norms that have passed the test of time tend to have strong survival traits. Tradition is to the human survival what capital is to the economy. However, methodological individualism frees the individual from subjugation to the constraints of tradition and morality. The individual is free to ignore some moral norms in the pursuit of his own preferences but he must bear the cost of his actions.

The capitalist community is then conceived as a voluntary association of utility-seeking individuals. The community has no predetermined outcome. Instead of the exogenously imposed idea of "good life," the emphasis in the capitalist community is on the *rule of the game* that allow each individual the freedom of choice and the obligation to bear the costs of pursuing his own preferences. Whatever outcome emerges from the interaction of utility-seeking individuals is clearly an unintended outcome. But as long as the rules of the game are fair, such an outcome must also be fair. As Hayek says, "Capitalism is an effective way of making man take part in a process more complex than he could comprehend, and it was through the free market that he contributed to ends which were not part of his purpose."

What classical liberals considered as the freeing of man from the constraints of religion and tradition, conservative Catholics saw as the erosion of morality and rejection of all "absolute" values upon which moral norms are centered. Conservative Catholic philosophy then raised the issue of *the legitimacy of capitalism as a moral system*.

The Catholic philosophy considers the community as an organic whole. Members of the community are expected to cooperate in the pursuit of the prescribed outcome (common good). The rules of the game in the community are adjusted to the requirements of the common good. The social preference function is consistent with the concept of "good life" and is enforced by laws, tradition, and moral teachings of the Church. With respect to the firm, the conservative Catholic philosophy emphasizes the organic unity of the enterprise in preference to individual self-interest; cooperation between workers, managers, and owners in preference to profit maximization; and a humane aspect of the process of production in preference to efficiency. Thus, the idea of some type of codetermination is a predictable outcome of its teaching.

The conservative Catholic philosophy rejects methodological individualism not because of its lack of interest in individual liberty, disregard for freedom of choice, and indifference to economic efficiency, but because the autonomy of individual choices in the free market does not necessarily generate *morally* satisfying sets of preferences. The fact is, however, that the free market does not generate preferences. It merely allows each and every individual to reveal his tastes whatever they might be. The conservative philosopher who argues against the liberty of individual choice which the capitalist system allows should direct his criticism toward the institutions—such as the educational establishment, the Church, the family, and the media—that form the preferences, rather than toward the free market in which those preferences are merely revealed.

Given individual preferences, there is positive moral content in the allocative outcome to which freedom of individual choice leads in an open-market, private property community. Morever, the capitalist system promotes the development of individuals, cultivates the strength from confronting risk, and puts a premium on the respect for promises. A reputation for honest dealing is a source of wealth. Competitive markets weed out crooks, cheaters, and liars. While the market does not make people moral (or immoral), it raises the cost of unethical behavior. Thus, the capitalist system has a strong moral content.

While the conservative Catholic philosophy criticized the free market for its alleged failure to generate morally satisfying sets of preferences, Marxists raised the issue of the rights of ownership. Their position is that *private property rights are a major cause of exploitation of man by man.* In pursuing this line of analysis, Marxists revived Marx's concept of alienated labor and made it the central issue in their criticism of capitalism. Marx's analysis of the concept of alienated labor can be summarized in four steps that lead to the fundamental premise that the right of ownership is the major source of class struggle and exploitation in capitalism. First, since it does not belong to him, the product of his labor appears to the worker as an alien object. Second, the worker is then alienated from his work. Instead of being a source of satisfaction, work activity becomes merely a means for subsistence. Third, the alienation of man from his product and from his work activity results in his alienation from those who have the right to appropriate the product of his hands. Fourth, the alienation of man from another man is, because men belong to distinct social classes, in effect the alienation of one social class (the proletariat) from another (property owners). The right of ownership is then the source of exploitation and class struggle in capitalism. To a Marxist, codetermination is a step in alleviating the alienation of labor.

Sources of Current Support

The extent to which workers support codetermination is not clear. Codetermination was soundly defeated in Switzerland, the only country in which the issue was put before the voting population. Various surveys conducted in Europe show that the employees have a greater interest in the functions of the Works Council than in codetermination. One reason for this lack of interest is that codetermination is removed from the employees' individual problems. In general, workers seem more interested in information about the performance of their firms than in actual involvement with decision-making processes.

Labor's relative indifference toward codetermination is not too surprising. Workers' interests lie in the rate of growth of their incomes, not in participatory democracy. And the negotiation of collective agreements has been the best understood and historically tested method for influencing economic and social status of labor. Workers' support for codetermination depends on the ability of those who are actively promoting labor participation in the decision-making process to demonstrate to laborers that participatory democracy is indeed an effective method for raising their total compensation.

The major support for codetermination in the West comes from two groups: the intellectual community and labor union leaders. Predictably, both groups argue that their support for codetermination stems from a genuine concern for the economic and social status of labor. However, the intellectuals, as well as union leaders, support codetermination for reasons that are consistent with their own private interests.

Codetermination is a vehicle through which the intellectual community seeks to restructure Western societies in ways that conform to its own perception of justice and equality. That is, the intellectuals want to obtain for labor what they think workers should want for themselves. It is important to distinguish, however, between those intellectuals who see codetermination as a vehicle for making capitalism a better system and those who look upon codetermination as a step in destroying it.

The first group of intellectuals looks upon the modern corporation as a political entity. This view of the modern corporation justifies the critics' insistence on democratic participation of owners, managers, and employees in the decision-making process. They see codetermination as a method for bestowing benefits on labor without any detrimental effect to stockholders.[7]

Another group of intellectuals that supports codetermination is the Marxists. They have revived Marx's criticism of capitalism that centers on the concept of alienated labor. Marxists support codetermination because it attenuates the right of ownership in resources. The following captures the essence of their position on codetermination:

> Only democracy and participation in production—i.e. the replacement of the capitalist class by the working class as the architects of production, and the accountability of managers and technicians to the will of workers—is compatible with equality and full individual development.[8]

The support of union leaders for codetermination is predicated on the right—an important property right—to select workers who sit on the board of directors of business firms. In the absence of such a right, labor leaders would have incentives to oppose codetermination. However, once they have been able to secure this right, as they did in Western Europe, codetermination becomes a vehicle through which labor leaders could increase their political and economic influence over the character of economic life. For union leaders, codetermination is a power issue which enhances the union power because the worker-board members are either affiliated or dominated by their unions. Predictably, business firms' decisions are likely to be made on the basis of internal politics rather than economic considerations.

The main advantage for labor unions lies in the area of information. With union representatives sitting on the board of directors of business firms, the union has access to all financial and technical data which it could use in planning and conducting collective bargaining.

American labor unions, on the other hand, have been less than enthusiastic about codetermination. For example, Lane Kirkland of the AFL-CIO was blunt in ruling labor unions' support for codetermination:

> The American worker is smart enough to know, in his bones, that salvation lies—not in reshuffling the chairs in the board room or the executive suite—but in the growing strength and bargaining power of his own autonomous organizations.[9]

These flat rejections by American union leaders of codetermination suggest that labor is not ready to substitute political decisions for collective bargaining on economic issues.

History of Codetermination in Germany

Codetermination in Germany finds its source in the philosophical origins of industrial democracy. As early as 1835, Professors Robert von Mohl, Wilhelm Roscher, and Bruno Hildebrand from the University of Tubingen proposed to create "workers' committees" in business firms. They felt that capitalism had failed to emphasize moral issues. Their proposal did not amount to actual codetermination at decision-making levels. The proposal was limited to giving labor the right of hearing. The emphasis was on moral appeals to conscience rather than legal changes.[10]

In 1848, the first elected German Parliament met in Frankfurt. Among other matters, the Parliament intended to pass legislation that was called *Reichsgewerbeordnung.* That was the first legislative effort to create representation of workers in business firms. According to German lawyer and codetermination expert Walter Kolvenbach, Article 3 of the *Reichsgewerbeordnung* is one of the most important developments for study of the history of the codetermination movement in Germany.[11]

The law did not pass but an interesting development occurred in subsequent years. Many provisions of *Reichsgewerbeordnung* were voluntarily implemented by a number of firms. The workers and the owners of business firms found it in their self-interest to work out mutually beneficial contractual agreements *without* resorting to the authority of the state. The point is, of course, that parties to a contract can identify opportunities for exchange, determine their own trade-offs (which are not likely to be the same for all firms), and negotiate terms of exchange at a lower cost than a third party could possibly do it for them. While law applies equally to all firms, voluntary contracts allow the owner and his workers to identify and exploit opportunities that are specific to their firm.

The voluntary emergence of contractual agreements within business firms was eventually arrested by the state. Worker committee laws were enacted in Bavaria in 1900 and in Prussia in 1905. Those laws began the process of exogenous changes in the employer-employee relationship. Instead of endogenous development of contractual agreements that could vary from one firm to another in accordance with their own specific problems, the state began to impose a set of uniform rules on all business firms.

The Constitution of 1919 incorporated the concept of codetermination in Article 165:

> The wage-earning and salaried employees are called upon the cooperate, with equal rights and in community with the entrepreneurs, on the regulation of wage and working conditions and on the total economic development of the productive forces.

In 1920, the Works Council law was enacted. It provided workers with the right of hearing in social and personnel questions. In 1922, a new law was passed. According to that law one or two employees must be seated on supervisory councils of business firms. *It was the first law on codetermination in Germany.* The development that began in 1848 with a proposal to establish workers' councils has eventually led to labor participation in the management of business firms.

During the Nazi years all laws on Works Councils and codetermination were abolished. In 1946, the Military Government passed the so-called Act 22 which reestablished Works Councils. In 1951, the law on the Codetermination of Employees on the Supervisory Boards and Boards of Management of Enterprises in the Coal Mining, Iron and Steel Producing Industry was enacted. The stage was then set for the current phase in the development of codetermination in Germany.

The framework of labor participation in the management of business firms in today's Germany is determined by the following three laws:

The Montan Act of 1951

The Works Constitution Act of 1952
(revised in 1972)

The Codetermination Act of 1976

Initially, the allies endorsed the idea of nationalizing the Montan industry (coal, iron, and steel). For political and social reasons the idea was eventually dropped and the Montan industry ended with a codetermination scheme. The stockholders and the employees were given an equal number of seats on the supervisory council. Labor unions dominated workers' representatives.

The first post-war elections in 1949 gave the conservatives (led by Adenauer) a substantial majority in the Parliament. Adenauer adopted the conservative philosophy regarding codetermination. He wanted to promote the codetermination model which emphasized the organic unity of the owners and the employees in business firms and rejected the claim of trade unions that they speak for labor. However, under the threat of strikes and after some heated political discussion in and out of the German Parliament, Adenauer had to work out a crompromise that preserved the union gains in the Montan industry.

The Montan Act of 1951 covers all firms in the mining and the iron and steel producing industries that employ at least 1,000 workers. The supervisory council of a firm in the Montan industry consists of eleven elected members.[12] The stockholders and the employees appoint four members each. In addition, the stockholders, as well as the employees, appoint an additional external member who cannot be a representative either of a union or of an employer organization nor can he be employed by that firm or otherwise connected with it in some economic way. The eleventh member is jointly elected by all supervisory board members.

The Works Constitution Act of 1952 is a clear expression of the conservative codetermination model. However, subsequent legal developments and in particular the Codetermination Act of 1976 have de-emphasized the role of conservative Catholic philosophy and strengthened the role of labor unions in the codetermination movement.

The Works Constitution Act of 1952 stipulates employees' rights at three different levels: the personal, the shop, and the decision-making levels of the firm.

On the personal level each employee is granted the right to information, hearing, and discussion of issues such as working conditions, hiring, firing, and layoffs. On the plant level, the act prescribes the institution of a *works council*. The works councils are elected by the employees and vary in size.

The works council's major functions are to propose measures that enhance the employees' welfare, to monitor existing collective bargaining agreements, social legislation, and other internal rules, and to receive complaints from the employees and negotiate their settlements with the employer. In general, the function of the worker council is to act as a social agent for the employees.

On the decision-making level of the firm, the Works Constitution Act stipulates that in firms that employ more than 500 people, one-third of the members of the supervisory council must consist of labor representatives. The employee representatives are directly elected by secret ballot. They are not appointed by labor unions. Thus, the Works Constitution Act introduced a type of codetermination that is consistent with the conservative Catholic philosophy.

The Codetermination Act of 1976 is a clear-cut departure from the conservative philosophy that considers the firm as the organic unity. The union leadership in Germany never accepted Adenauer's codetermination model of 1952. It continued to press for the extension of the Montan model to the entire German industry. The Act of 1976 represents a definite victory for German trade unions' and neo-Marxists' position on the role of codetermination in the West.

The Codetermination Act of 1976 applies to all business firms that have more than 2,000 employees (about 470 firms). The Supervisory Board has 12 members. Of these 12, six are representatives of the shareholders and six are representatives of the employees. In firms which employ more than 10,000 workers, the supervisory board may have the maximum of twenty members with an equal distribution of seats between the shareholders and the employees.

Recent Experiences in Germany

It is too early to evaluate economic and social consequences of codetermination in Germany. The evidence is far from complete. Yet some problems have already surfaced, the nature of which suggest that not only is codetermination costly as a method of organizing production but also it is a vehicle for the transfer of wealth from the shareholders to labor unions and employees of business firms.

After the passage of the Montan Act of 1951 many business firms tried to escape the parity representation on the supervisory board *via* mergers, reorganization and other structural changes. Such an escape would make them subject only to the one-third employee representatives requirement of the Works Constitution Act. German trade unions successfully fought such attempts by business firms to escape the legal requirements of the Montan Act in the parliament, in the courts, and through the use of various special "agreements" (i.e., power plays) with individual firms. The same situation occurred after the enactment of the Codetermination Act of 1976. A large number of firms tried to avoid being subject to this law; the result was that the Act which was expected to apply to about 620 firms eventually applied to only about 470 enterprises, evidence that codetermination is harmful to the shareholders.

There are many problems with the practice of codetermination. For instance, the election procedure has taken up to 56 weeks. Companies have spent millions of marks for travel expenses, printing costs and the loss of working hours. Another cost is associated with the fact that the supervisory board consists of two groups: the shareholders' representatives and the employees' representatives. The result is that prior to the official meetings of the board separate sessions have to be held by those two groups to work out their respective positions. Thus, the discussions in the board room are not really free exchanges of thoughts, ideas, and judgements but a sort of bargaining between the two sides. A case in point would be Volkswagen's decision to open a plant in the United States. The decision was delayed for over two years due to a costly political debate, as economic decisions were opposed by union political control.

The question of conflict of interests has also surfaced. The management is supposed to give the supervisory board all the information about the firm. The members of the supervisory board are, in turn, expected to keep information secret. However, representatives of labor unions feel that when it comes to jobs, wages, and workers' welfare, their obligation to employees supersedes any secrecy obligation.[13] This was the case in many firms such as Volkswagen and AEG. Also, if a union can (thorugh its representatives on the board) arm itself with critical information about the firm, it would have a serious advantage in wage negotiations and other decisions.

Codetermination and Property Rights

Economic activity involves social interaction at two levels. The first level involves the development, specification, and modification of property rights by which the community seeks to resolve social problems that have their source in economic activity. Property rights define the *rules of the game*. Changes in property rights are changes in the rules of the game.

Writing on the concept of property rights, I. Fisher said:

> A property right is the liberty or permit to enjoy benefits of wealth while assuming the costs which those benefits entail . . . Property rights, unlike wealth or benefits, are not physical objects nor events, but are abstract social relations. A property right is not a thing.[14]

Property rights are defined as the sanctioned behavioral relations *among men* (such as laws, regulations, and customs) that arise from the existence of scarce goods and which pertain to their use. The set of property relations, which describe the position of each individual with respect to the utilization of scarce resources defines the general character of social and economic life in the community, thus defining the country's economic system. Individuals respond to incentives, and the pattern of incentives present at any time is influenced by the prevailing property rights structures.

The second level of social activity involves decision-making—individual choices and contracts (exchanges) within the prevailing property rights structures. People seek contracts and negotiate terms of exchange expecting to reach a higher level of satisfaction. Thus, the second level of social activity is concerned with maximizing the behavior of individuals and with the allocation and use of resources. Importantly, the prevailing property relations determine the extent of contractual (exchange) activities.

Codetermination affects both levels of social activity. That is, the effects of codetermination are not limited to marginal adjustments within the system. Labor participation in the management of business firms changes the prevailing property relations between the shareholders, managers, employees, and labor unions; it affects the institutional structures. The analysis of codetermination must then identify changes in property rights structures and establish their effects on the rules of the game before turning to the question of how the game is played.

In the real world, institutional structures cannot be assumed to be unchanging. As new property rights develop and as the old ones are modified the country's institutions change. The issue is the analysis of the consequences of changes in property rights that could be attributed to the laws of codetermination.

The laws on codetermination trigger institutional restructuring that is exogenous to the system. The laws change the prevailing relationship between the shareholders, managers, employees, and labor unions. Consequently, they affect the location of decision-making powers, appropriability of rewards, and the relationship between risk taking and bearing of costs in labor participatory firms. Through those effects, the laws change the way the game is played, especially managerial decisions, wage negotiations, vector of labor compensation (fringe benefits, share of profit, contractual wage, etc.), employment policies, and equity financing. Proponents of codetermination use the government to pass legislation that results in a politically determined transfer of wealth from one group of people to another. The relevant issue for economic analysis is to look into the effects of the institutional restructuring on the allocation and use of resources in the community. For every aspect of the market that is touched by new rules must cause distortions in the allocation of resources.

Laws on codetermination do not emerge in response to the requirement for new contractual forms. In a capitalist society we observe a large number of different types of firms such as single proprietorship, partnerships, cooperatives, not-for-profit firms, and corporations. All these firms have emerged through voluntary contractual negotiations and survived competition from other types of firms. In fact, capitalism generates a selection process among various types of firms that is consistent with economic efficiency. Different types of firms seem to survive in different markets. Partnerships appear more efficient in labor intensive industries such as law, while the corporate firms are more likely to survive in capital intensive industries.

The crucial evidence is that the codetermining firm has not emerged voluntarily in the West; it has not survived by demonstrating its superiority over competing types of firms. There is no law in the United States or Western Europe that prohibits codetermination. If that type of organization were really efficient it would have been negotiated voluntarily. The very fact that the government has to mandate the codetermining firm and protect it from competition is evidence of its inefficiency.

The Allocation of Resources

Whatever the facade of words, a major purpose of codetermination is to bring about redistribution of income. Emotion-charged terms such as "industrial democracy" and "labor participation" are merely code words for using the political system to secure wealth transfers. The argument that under codetermination productivity of labor will increase in response to changes in workers' total compensation and reduced alienation destroys the case for codetermination that is mandated by law.

Codetermination shifts the responsibility for decisions to a group of people who are not at all affected by the consequences of the decisions. No matter what the outcome of the decision is, the worker receives contractual wages—his risk is limited. Codetermination puts stockholders into an uninviting situation—if the corporation makes an investment decision that is successful, the gains are shared with labor. If, on the other hand, the investment decision is not successful, stockholders alone bear the losses. Codetermination violates the risk-reward relationship which, in turn, must raise the cost (reduce the supply) of equity capital.

Economic analysis of codetermination presupposes a "political" model capable of explaining the behavior of the board of directors, the affects of majority-voting on the management of business firms, and the perception of the average worker concerning the relationship between his work effort and rewards from labor participation in the decision process.

It follows that economic analysis of codetermination faces a serious problem just getting off the ground. The best we can do at this time is to identify social institutions that codetermination tends to affect and infer some predictable behavioral effects of labor participation on the allocation of resources.

The freedom of contract and the right of ownership are, as it was said earlier, two fundamental institutions of capitalism which are endangered by forced codetermination.

Forced codetermination restricts individuals' freedom to negotiate the most beneficial organizational forms. The freedom of contract means that labor participation in corporate management could emerge out of voluntary contractual arrangements as have many other types of firms. Indeed, there are cases in which codetermination has emerged voluntarily. If codetermination raises the firm's productivity or bestows benefits on labor in excess of stockholders' costs, why do we need laws on codetermination?

Codetermination also interferes with the right of ownership. Labor participation in the management of business firms implies the political action of granting labor a voice in areas of decision-making that have traditionally been the prerogative of ownership, either directly or through hired representatives (e.g. managers). What is important to bear in mind is that current decisions about the use of resources have future consequences (measured by changes in the value of resources). Different property rights arrangements imply different assignments of benefits and losses from current decisions. In a private property capitalist economy the owner bears all the future consquences of his (or hired representatives') current decisions.

Codetermination causes a separation between decision-making and risk bearing.[15] In a codetermining firm those who participate in decision-making processes do not bear *all* changes in the value of the firm's assets. Codetermination then attentuates the right of ownership. Attenuation of ownership means a change in the quality of decisions. Given the worker's time horizon, which is limited to their expected employment by the firm, the labor participatory firm has more incentives to choose investment alternatives and business politicies that shift incomes forward and postpone costs. For example, consider two investment alternatives of equal costs. The expected present value of one alternative is $1,000 while the other yields only $750. However, if the returns from the first alternative are discounted over a period of 20 years and those of the second over only five years, workers could easily push the management in the direction of choosing the less profitable one. Even in the absence of sharing in the firm's profits, wage negotiations and their perception of job security would provide workers with incentives to prefer business policies that promise larger annual earnings over a limited time period to those policies that maximize the firm's worth.

If codetermination means a transfer of wealth from the shareholders to labor we can predict the following chain of events. The rate of return from capital invested in labor participatory firms (mostly corporations) will fall. The resulting flight of capital into the other (non-participatory) alternatives such as small firms, human capital, bonds, foreign investment will change investment patterns in the economy. The rate of capital formations in the corporate sector will be smaller and in other areas greater than it would otherwise be. The rate of return in non-participatory investments will fall while the marginal productivity of labor will fall. In equilibrium, corporate firms will produce smaller outputs and charge higher prices than they would otherwise. Conversely, prices will be lower and outputs greater in non-participatory sectors of the economy. If this simple scenario is predictive of the general effects of codetermination, labor participation in the management of business firms will result in the reallocation of resources away from the most efficient, technically advanced and productive sector of the economy and toward less efficient, technically less capable and less productive alternatives. A general decline of the level and character of the economy, could then be predicted.

Codetermination is a costly political reform. Let us now summarize some conspicuous costs of codetermination:[16]

1. *Monopoly in the market for business organizations.* There is no law in the United States or Western Europe that prohibits codetermination. If that type of organization were really efficient, it would have emerged contractually. The fact that the law has to mandate the codetermining firm, and to protect it from competition by other types of firms, is evidence of its relative inefficiency.

2. *Increased cost of equity capital.* The fact that stockholders must be forced by law to accept codetermination is the best evidence that they are adversely affected by it. Labor representatives on the board of directors represent those who have no claim on the capitalized value of assets. A major consequence has to be a higher cost of equity capital to offset lower returns to the holders of stocks and bonds.

3. *Changes in the pattern of investment.* Labor representatives on the board of directors have incentives to push for investment decisions that promise to maximize near term cash flow.

4. *Reallocation of resources.* An increase in the cost of equity capital means that the average rate of return in labor participating firms will fall. The result will be a shift of capital toward non-participatory alternatives such as smaller firms, human capital and foreign investments.

Codetermination in California

As it was suggested earlier in this study, codetermination in Western Europe and codetermination introduced by the California Labor Relations Act are substantially different. In Western Europe, labor representatives on the board of directors participate jointly with other directors in the decision-making process at the firm's level. Under the California Labor Relations Act (hereafter CALRA) a significant amount of decision-making power is simply transferred to labor unions. According to Cottle et al., CALRA has made it possible for labor unions to: assign jobs to union members, allow or forbid field workers to be retained by the employer for more than one growing season, require workers to donate to selected political organizations, establish the type of pesticides to be used on crops, impose research restrictions on the universities in California on the development of labor-saving machinery, and, under the good standing rule, tell individual farms which workers may be hired. CALRA has placed many management prerogatives in the domain of labor unions—but not of labor. It has significantly reduced the opportunity set of the management in the agri-business. For example, the union's right to enforce the good standing rule and to forbid a worker's right to negotiate his employment with an employer leads one to question whether individual workers in the agri-business in California are now freer than they were before CALRA. Rather than joining the management as is the case in Western Europe, labor unions in the agri-business in California can dictate to it.

According to Cottle et. al., the labor union in the agri-business in California has enough power to control the rate of output and to appropriate monopoly profits.

Conclusion

This study is an attempt to trace the history and development of codetermination in Western Europe and to assess its economic, political, and social consequences. The study concentrates on the codetermination movement in Germany because that country has been the undisputed leader in promoting various codetermination schemes.

The idea of codetermination is not a recent phenomenon. It arose from naive but serious misconceptions about the nature of capitalism. Predictably, the actual implementation of labor participation has generated the consequences that deviate from the intentions of its ideological founders.

Economic consequences of codetermination are misallocation of resources, redistribution of income, reduced supply of equity capital, and changes in the pattern of investment. Economic consequences of codetermination are traceable to using political mechanism rather than market mechanism in solving practical economic problems. The unions' rise to power is a major political consequence of codetermination. Most importantly, codetermination has failed to emerge out of voluntary contracts as have many other organizational forms. The result is that codetermination has to be mandated by law. Social consequences of forced codetermination, then, are easy to identify. Forced codetermination *restricts* individuals' freedom to seek and negotiate mutuall preferred contractual arrangements and *attenuates* the right of ownership in capital goods. Social consequences of codetermination represent a major departure from capitalism. Codetermination does not merely weaken capitalism—it attacks capitalism at its very roots.

Notes

1. The supervisory board is the controlling body of the firm—like the board of directors in the United States.

2. *Democratie Francaise,* October 1976.

3. M. Kreifels, "Codetermination in Germany," Conference on Codetermination, Ditchley Park, May 1980, p. 8.

4. "Employee Participation and Company Structure in the European Community," *Bulletin of the European Communities,* August 1975, p. 9.

5. "The Battle over Codetermination," *The Wall Street Journal,* August 10, 1977.

6. A. Alchian, *Private Rights to Property: The Basis of Corporate Governance and Human Rights* (forthcoming).

7. E. Batstone, "Industrial Democracy and Worker Representation at Board Level: A Review of the European Experience," *Industrial Democracy: European Experience.* Industrial Democracy Committee Research Report. London, Her Majesty's Stationery Office, 1976, p. 43.

8. H. Gintis, "Welfare Economics and Individual Development: A Reply to Talcott Persons," *Quarterly Journal of Economics,* 89, May 1975, p. 301-2.

9. J. Ellenberger, "The Realities of Codetermination," *AFL-CIO Federationist,* October 1977.

10. See H. Monissen, "Labor Participation in the Management of Business Firms in Germany," in S. Pejovich (ed.), *The Codetermination Movement in the West,* Lexington, Mass.: Lexington Books, D.C. Heath and Company, 1978; and H. Tenteberg. Geschichte der Industriellen Mitbestimmung in Deutschland, Tubingen, 1961.

11. W. Kolvenbach, "Codetermination in Germany," Unpublished paper, pp. 2-3.

12. Business firms with capital assets in excess of 20 million DM may appoint 15 members to their supervisory councils. If capital assets of a firm exceed 50 million DM the firm may have the maximum of 21 members on its supervisory council.

13. M. Paul, "Germany's Requiring of Workers on Boards Causes Many Problems," *The Wall Street Journal,* Dec. 10, 1979, pp. 1 and 29.

14. I. Fisher, *Elementary Principles of Economics,* New York: Macmillan, 1923, p. 27.

15. See S. Pejovich, "Codetermination: Labor Participation in Management," *Modern Age,* Winter 1978, p. 36.

16. S. Pejovich, "The Costs of Codetermination," *Review of Social Economy,* December 1980.

17. R. Cottle, H. Macaulay, and B. Yandle. *Government Regulation of Wages and Conditions of Work: The Case of the California Labor Relations Act,* College Station: Texas A&M University Press, forthcoming. To the best of my knowledge, this work is the only one on the subject of forced codetermination in the United States.

9 Sweden at the End of the Middle Way

Ingemar Ståhl

Introduction

During the main part of the postwar period Sweden has been looked upon as an interesting case and even as an example worth following with regard to the combination of a high economic-growth rate and a comprehensive welfare system. The Swedish welfare state has thus to a certain extent been an intellectual challenge to those who have considered that it would be difficult to combine a high economic-growth rate with a large amount of government or political intervention in the economy.

This chapter will analyze this paradox. For reasons that will be obvious the analysis is divided into two main periods, the first starting at the beginning of the 1930s and ending at the time of the first oil crisis and the second period covering the recent years. During the first period the Social Democratic Labour party was in government, either alone or leading a coalition with the Farmers party (except for a very broad coalition covering also Liberals and Conservatives during the period of the Second World War); during the second period (since 1976) the government has consisted of the three nonsocialist parties (the former Farmers party now called the Centre party, the Liberal party, and the Conservative party).

The 1970s constitute now only a political watershed with a forty-four-year uninterrupted period of the Social Democratic party leading the central government ending in 1976, but also an economic watershed. The Swedish growth experience had been very good, generally far above the average of the Organization for Economic Cooperation and Development (OECD) countries until 1970. The growth experience during the 1970s put Sweden far below the average. There is a manifest economic crisis with a deficit in current accounts of 5 percent of gross domestic product (GDP) and a deficit in the budget of the central government exceeding 10 percent of GDP. Inflation rate is among the highest in the OECD area, industrial production has been at a standstill since 1974, and the total size of the public sector (consumption, investments, and transfers) has reached the almost incredible figure of 65 percent of GDP. A devaluation of the Swedish currency is expected, and the inflation rate will soar.

How could it happen? Is it just a coincidence of unlucky circumstances created by the oil crisis? If so, why should other heavily oil-importing countries behave much better? Another possible explanation is that the Swedish industrial structure was extremely vulnerable for the relative price changes that followed the oil crisis. An export sector depending on iron-ore shipyards, steel, automobiles, and engineering goods for investment was a favorable combination for the high-growth period of the 1960s. Although the industrial structure was not adapted to the new market conditions of the 1970s, the obvious counterquestions are, Why have there not been adaptive changes during the 1970s, and why is a deindustrialized process still going on?

A third category of explanations points to the fact that the Swedish unit-labor costs have risen considerably particularly during 1975 to 1976 and 1979 to 1980. In combination with a policy of fixed exchange rates, this has created an overvalued currency. Wage costs are to a large extent endogenous in the economic system, and the problem will thus be an internal problem of why wage-cost inflation has been a characteristic feature of the Swedish economy and why the positive effects of export and industrial production of the devaluatins in 1977 ceased in 1979 and 1980. A highly possible feature of the Swedish labor market has been its relative stability and low strike rate. Even this is no longer true with a combination of strikes and lockouts covering large parts of both the private and public sectors during the wage negotiations in the spring of 1980.

This chapter brings forward the hypothesis of the *arteriosclerotic economy* being the long-run result of increasing political interventions in the market and the growth of interest groups with the possibility of blocking decisions or delaying adjustments. The main feature in this development has been an expansion of the areas for political decision making (with a majority decision rule) and the decrease of market decisions.

The Growth Experience

When industrialization started in Sweden in the 1870s, the country was an underdeveloped agricultural economy. Traditional export products from earlier periods—tar, iron, and copper—no longer played any role after the technical changes that had taken place in the early stages of the industrial revolution. The Swedish development was to a large extent an almost classical example of export-led growth. It started in the 1850s with export of oats to England—oats being an essential fuel for the two hundred fifty thousand horses covering the streets of London with manure. The building boom in England further created a demand for timber. During the last decades of the nineteenth century Sweden became the largest timber-export country in the world market.

Industrialization continued with pulp industry and steel industry using imported coal instead of domestic charcoal, and the new Thomas-process for steel production made the iron ore deposits in northern Sweden an important economic asset. One interesting feature in the industrialization process was the creation at an early stage of a number of still existing firms in the engineering industry, based partly on Swedish innovations or Swedish adaptions of foreign technology. During the same period some of the still most important commercial banks were created.

The role of government in this process was very limited. Except for the main lines in the railway system, the expansion took place as a handbook example of export-led growth under capitalistic market conditions. The insignificant role of government in the industrial sector was a characteristic feature until the 1970s. Sweden never had a nationalization similar to that in the United Kingdom immediately after the war. It is likely that very important features of the success story were the predominantly private export-oriented industrial sector and a government policy of free international trade. This was an important part of the system of *rules of the game* governing Swedish economy for a long time. Although nationalization was a point of principle in the program of the Social-Democrat party, the question remained as an internal point of discussion that never led to political actions.

As has already been stated the growth of internationally oriented engineering corporations (with smaller subcontractors in Sweden) was an important feature of the growth process. Most of the ten largest firms were created before the First World War or during the interwar period: ASEA (heavy electric equipment), SKF (roller bearings), LM Ericsson (telephones and later electronics), Alfa-Laval (dairy equipment), Atlas Copco (motors and later pneumatic equipment), Bofors (guns and heavy engineering), and AGA (automatic lighthouses) were all started in an early stage of the industrialization period and have grown to international firms with in some cases most of the production outside Sweden. From the interwar period came Volvo (cars) and Electrolux (refrigerators, vacuum cleaners), and from the Second World War SAAB (aircraft and cars). Other important firms such as Swedish Match and Sandvik (special steel and alloys) also belong to the early phase. The same holds true for the raw-material industries (ore, steel, pulp, and paper) although there has been a considerable number of mergers as returns to scale have increased.

The backbone of the Swedish industry thus has been made out of private corporations operating in international markets and depending on a policy of free trade and competition. Industrial policy—if it ever was formulated in more exact terms—was until about 1970 limited to mainly two major government procurement programs of advanced technology: aircraft development for the air force and nuclear-power development. In both cases development took place at private firms (SAAB and ASEA) and not at government research facilities. The state ownership and management of railways, post and telecommunications, and about 40 percent of hydroelectric power was characterized more by technical professional ethics than political considerations.

The dynamic Swedish industry created in a capitalistic environment thus can be seen as the main factor behind the development process. Political decision making did not interfere with the basic allocation mechanisms but was more geared to redistributing the gains and in some cases also compensating the losers of a fast development process, combined with considerable structural changes. As will be discussed later some parts of the welfare schemes might even have had a positive effect on the allocation process by facilitating mobility of labor.

Table 9-1 gives the long-term growth rates for Sweden and some of the most important industrial economies. The relatively good Swedish growth performance over almost a century is reinforced if one looks at the growth rates in GDP per capita (table 9-2). Only Japan had a higher growth rate than Sweden measured over the whole period from 1870 to 1964.

An interesting feature is the acceleration of the growth rate during the postwar period that coincides with the main building up of the welfare state. However, table 9-3 shows that the experience from the last decade is fundamentally changed.

Labor Markets, Trade Unions, and Labor-Market Policy

By international standards the Swedish labor market is thoroughly unionized. Until recently it has shown few of the features characteristic of highly unionized labor markets. Strike rates have been exceptionally low, and inflation was for a

Table 9-1
Growth Rate in Gross Domestic Product from 1870 to 1970

	1870–1964	1870–1913	1913–1950	1950–1970
Sweden	2.8	3.0	2.2	4.0
Japan	3.9	3.3	–	9.5
United States	3.6	4.3	2.9	3.0
United Kingdom	1.9	2.2	1.7	2.8
Germany	2.8	2.9	1.2	6.3

Table 9-2
Growth Rate in Gross Domestic Product per Capita

	1870–1964	1870–1913	1913–1950	1950–1970
Sweden	2.1	2.3	1.6	3.3
Japan	2.7	2.3	–	8.3
United States	1.9	2.2	1.7	2.1
United Kingdom	1.2	1.3	1.3	2.2
Germany	1.8	1.8	0.4	5.3
France	1.5	1.4	0.7	4.2

Table 9–3
Growth Rate in Gross Domestic Product from
1965 to 1979

	1965–1973	1973–1979
Sweden	3.2	1.9
Japan	10.7	4.1
United States	3.7	2.4
United Kingdom	3.1	1.1
Germany	4.3	2.4

long time kept close to an international average. The Swedish exchange rate was actually stable (compared with the U.S. dollar) from 1949 to 1970 when the Bretton Woods system ceased to function. One major explanation behind this stability is probably the combination of an all-encompassing trade-union movement with negotiations taking place at a central level between the central organization of trade unions and the employers federation. Negative external effects of monopolistic behavior of one local or industry union on other trade-union members were thus internalized within the whole trade-union movement which could deter them from separate actions. The possibility of escalation from local labor-market conflicts to nationwide conflicts on a large scale might also have played a role somewhat comparable to nuclear deterrence. (A strike of a key group could in principle be met by a lockout directed against weak groups.) It is even perhaps true that highly centralized negotiations will come closer to a free-market solution than a market with monopolistic trade unions limited to certain areas or industries.

It was also a policy of the trade-union movement during the 1950s and the 1960s to reach something close to relative equilibrium wages. This policy was facilitated by a labor-market policy geared into increasing regional and industrial mobility mainly through retraining programs. Unemployment insurance played a minor role, and most labor-market policy programs were deliberately oriented toward retraining, mobility assistance, or temporary relief work. The role of active labor-market policy might have been overestimated as a way of increasing mobility and structural changes. The crucial point was probably that trade unions accepted changes and the labor-market policy compensated the losers. This picture has gradually changed during the last decade. In 1973—just before the election—a new bill on security in employment was passed, giving strict rules of seniority, in principle indefinite employment, and prolonged waiting times for dismissals in case of slack labor demand. This had a tendency to move unemployment into the firms and led to disastrous effects in the recession of 1975 to 1977. The policy shifted from mobility to preservation of jobs. At about the same time new laws on trade-union participation in enterprise decisions and trade-union representation on the board of directors were introduced. New work-environment legislation was added. It is no exaggeration to say that essential parts of the contract structure in the labor market were changed in the same years as the first oil crisis occurred.

The labor-market programs shifted to fewer mobility-oriented programs with, for example, training of slack labor within the firm under a recession. Loss of employment under the new labor-market laws also meant a loss of seniority, and trade-union policy shifted as well in favor of preserving old industries and blocking structural changes. During the crisis in 1975 to 1977 this led to heavy subsidization of shipyards, steelworks, and the textile industry. The new nonsocialist government in 1976 started in a situation with a clearly overvalued Swedish currency and rising unemployment. It could easily have been a political disaster with high unemployment rates during the first year of the new government. It saw that its only possible political option was to increase subsidies. Finally the government took over the three largest steelworks and merged them into one state-owned company. The same procedure took place in shipbuilding and textiles. Some of the cooperative firms in pulp and paper were saved from bankruptcy by a partial government takeover. It is an ironic feature that the nonsocialist government succeeded in nationalizing more enterprises in two to three years than the labor government did during forty-four years. Particularly in shipbuilding the new state enterprise has turned out to be a lame duck with negative value added and strong political pressure to keep employment within the firm and avoid structural changes.

With government intervention to preserve enterprises and employment, a large safety net was erected for taking care of the victims of inflationary wage increases. Together with a political acceptance of deficits in current accounts and a corresponding government borrowing from abroad and an increase of central-government deficits this meant that some basic rules of the game of the Swedish economy were changed. Noninterference in private business (with a few mainly regional exceptions) had been a tacit political rule which was abruptly violated. The new contract structure in the labor market can be interpreted to mean a higher natural rate of unemployment, with, for example, longer search times. Unemployment was suppressed by industrial subsidies and by an increase in labor market programs, thus giving permanent sheltered employment and finally an expansion of early retirement subsidized through the pension system. Open unemployment never exceeded 2.5 percent of the labor force, but if one includes different employment programs and sheltered industries, any figure at the level of 6 to 8 percent is easy to justify. Employment creation played an increasing role for the expansion of the public sector.

The wage policy of the trade-union movement has gradually also shifted during the period towards a policy of solidaristic wages. The main content of this policy is a stress on more egalitarian wage setting. The main problems are a faster closing down of old industries (for example, the textile industry) as

wage differential are smaller say between textile industry and engineering industry in Sweden than in Germany. The closing downs are then partly met by
government subsidies. Another problem—obviously not typical for Sweden—
are the relatively high wages for young workers and relatively low wages for
skilled and experienced workers, thus creating youth unemployment at the
same time as a shortage of skilled workers. The obvious remedies within a
political economy have been extensive training programs and public employment for the younger groups.

The Development of the Welfare State

Sweden was rather late in the development of the modern democratic institutions. When industrialization started in the 1870s the country had just changed
from a parliament of four estates (1866) to a two-chamber parliament that still
had a highly limited electorate and an allocation of votes according to income
and wealth. In the first elections to the new parliament, less than 20 percent of
the male population were eligible to vote. In local elections the eligible citizens
got a number of votes proportional to taxable wealth. In 1911 there was universal suffrage for men, and suffrage was extended to women in 1921.

The first reforms of a social-welfare type were obviously inspired by the
developments in Germany. In 1913 the first bill regarding a general old-age
pension was passed. Basic pensions of a rather small amount were given to all
citizens above sixty-seven years of age. (In present prices the annual pension was
$200). A year later government subsidies were given to unemployment funds.
In 1918 a law was passed regarding compulsory insurance for work accidents.
By standards of contemporary Europe this was not much of a social-welfare
state. A couple of years earlier government subsidies were allocated to private
sickness-insurance funds.

Almost no new reforms took place during the 1920s. In the 1930s there was
considerable growth of different welfare programs although the financial effects
were rather limited. The general tendency was to substitute social welfare based
on a means test with more general programs. In successive steps a from-the-
cradle-to-the-grave social-welfare program was built. Two parallel tendencies
can be observed. One was the creation of different transfer systems or social-
insurance systems. The other was the provision of social services. Education,
health services, day-care centers, and homes for the aged mainly were provided
free or at low out-of-pocket costs by agencies or organizations run mostly by
local government.

The main parts of the transfer and social-insurance systems are children's
allowances (regardless of income), income-related housing benefits, sick-pay
insurance, a comprehensive system for grants and loans for college and university students, unemployment insurance (which as an exception still is run by

trade unions but with 90 percent government subsidies), the basic pension system combined with special housing benefits to the old, and finally the supplementary income-related pension system.

Almost 100 percent of schools are run by local authorities, but there is central-government control of the curriculum. Schools are tax financed, and there are no tuition fees. Health care is run in a similar way by the county authorities with a very small private sector. (Of eighteen thousand doctors less than a thousand work as private physicians). Universities have no tuition fees and are coordinated in a nationwide system with parliament making the overall budget decisions.

A booming program at present is the extension of highly subsidized day-care centers administered by the municipal authorities. The subsidization level is incredible as the subsidy of one child might reach the level of ten thousand dollars (U.S. currency) per year.

A typical feature of the Swedish system is a tendency toward uniformity: all schools have the same curriculum; there is almost a military master plan for the health-care services; and so forth. It should also be stressed that the building up of the system has been gradual—often starting with a basic introduction bill with small economic impacts and then a gradual increase up to the present levels. Bureaucratic coordination rather than competition is also a trademark of the system.

With the growing impact of trade unions on the public sector this has obviously created new problems. Some recent studies indicate, for example, that productivity per man hour might have decreased by as much as 30 percent in the health-care system during the 1970s. Groups with strong vested interests in the present system have thus been created. The municipal workers' union is at present the largest trade union; this place was traditionally held by the metalworkers' union, which mainly had its members in export-oriented industry.

This fact in combination with the rapid expansion of the social-service sectors—partly due to the bad productivity performance—has probably had an important effect on wage formation. Traditionally, those in the export-oriented sectors were wage leaders, and the domestic sheltered sectors followed later. With a decline in industry—partly caused by excessive wage claims—and a fast-growing public sector the roles have been reversed with the public or rather local-government sectors as wage leaders.

It is here very easy to create a vicious circle: wages start going up in the public sector, and the export sector follows, but with fixed exchange rates employment will decline. In the first round this even creates a further expansion of the public sector as new jobs are created to keep unemployment down. A trade deficit occurs, and temporary equilibrium is created by a devaluation, which starts an inflationary process with compensatory claims from the trade unions in the public sector, who never experienced a slack in the demand. Then the process can start over once again. In the process there are also critical political components. Persons employed in the public sector or depending on government subsidies are increasing their share of the electorate at the same time as public employees have a very strong tendency to be overrepresented in political assemblies at all levels. It seems to be a gradual process in which the market is losing all the time and the public sector and its employees are the constant winners.

The symbiotic life among politicians, bureaucrats, and adminstrators reinforces this pressure upwards. Politicians elected to the county councils, which have the main responsiblity for health care, are elected because of their positive interest in expanding the health-care system (or at least the parts situated in their constituencies). Administrators with their monopoly situations with regard to information and formulation of issues and proposals have also strong interests in expansion. The countervailing powers are extremely weak, and with central government to a large extent financing local government by cost sharing, coordination between expenditure decisions and financing decisions is lacking.

A rough measure of the size of the welfare state will be the total taxes in relation to GDP (see table 9–4). When looking at this table one should remember that the total public budgets were balanced or even had a financial surplus (with the supplementary pension fund lending to the semipublic-housing sector and the private-industrial sector) and that the total government deficits started to grow in the 1970s. It should also be observed that the rate of diminishing the private sector has been increasing. In 1950, 79 percent of GDP was outside the taxes. Nontaxed share of GDP decreased to 75 percent in 1955, that is, a decrease of 5 percent. From 1975 to 1979 the nontaxed share decreased from 53 to 48 percent, that is, a decrease of almost 10 percent. It is of some interest to observe that the first nonsocialist government in forty-four years almost introduced a quantum jump in the relative importance of the public sector, in particular when the total deficits are considered.

If one looks at the composition of the total public sector, about 29 percent of GDP is public consumption. The sectors dominated by central government—defense, justice and crime prevention, research and university education, and

Table 9–4
Taxes as a Share of Gross Domestic Product

	Percent
1950	20.9
1955	24.9
1960	28.7
1965	35.0
1970	40.0
1975	46.9
1979	52.0

finally the national road system—share 8 percent of GDP. These sectors that are rather close to a theoretical concept of collective goods have shown rather small growth rates. The budget cuts at present proposed by the central government concern those sectors responsible for health, schools, and care of children and the old in different types of institutions. These sectors take 21 percent of GDP. During the last decade the growth rate for local government was more than twice as high as the growth in GDP. However, one may doubt if there were any significant increases in production at all in some of the sectors as health and education.

The transfer system redistributes something close to 31 percent of GDP. The remaining 5 percent to reach the level of a public-sector share of GDP of 65 percent are investments in the public sector. It should be observed that the genuine collective sectors and an income redistribution to individuals who are congenitally disabled are rather small; probably less than 10 percent of GDP. This is in a certain sense the true size of the welfare state. The remaining part could be supplied by the private sector combined with private insurance and in some cases a combination of loans and savings plans. One might even doubt that there is much income redistribution—compared with a system of private insurance and savings and loan schemes. As will be discussed later, the political solution with high marginal taxes and lump-sum transfers might have caused large distortions and inefficiencies.

The Tax System

As was already mentioned the total public expenditure (public consumption, investments, and transfers) reached a record figure in 1979 of 65.4 percent of total GDP.[1] If one looks at the income side, taxes including payroll taxes or premiums for the social-insurance system covered 52 percent of GDP; other sources of income (as nominal interest income in the supplementary pension fund, fees for some public services, and imputed income on public capital) accounted for another 9.6 percent; and finally a total financial surplus in the pension fund was of the size of 3.4 percent. However, added to this there should be another 2.5 percent of GDP that was borrowed in the capital markets by central government and then lent out to firms and households, partly as a result of growing state intervention in industry. To raise 52 percent of GDP as taxes creates considerable problems. There are no hidden sources available, and with the distribution between profits and wages, the main tax source must be wage income or private consumption.

The main components of the tax system are the progressive-rates income tax and the proportional taxes to counties and municipalities (including parish tax to the state church), the value-added tax (VAT), and a payroll tax which formally consists of a number of special social-insurance premiums and payroll taxes. In addition, there are a number of excise taxes on alcohol, tobacco, oil, gasoline, and electric energy. Of minor significance from a purely financial point of view are the wealth tax, the capital-gains tax, and the corporate tax. However, these taxes might have large incentive and allocation effects. Formally the social-insurance premiums and the payroll taxes are added to the negotiated salaries and, thus, hidden from the income earners (except for the self-employed). The total rate is at present about 35 percent, of which twelve percentage units are for the supplementary pension scheme and eleven percentage units for the sickness-payment insurance. In these two cases there are special budgets. The remaining twelve percentage units go into the public budget although many of the components have fancy names depending on the specific reform that they were intended to finance at the time of introduction. (There is thus a day-care-center tax as well as an adult-education tax although there are two special budgets for these purposes.)

A 35 percent payroll tax is equal to 26 percent tax on the total wage cost. The income tax is applied to wage incomes (after payroll tax) as well as capital income, capital gains (defined in a specific way), and business income (after deduction of an equivalent of the payroll tax). Wage incomes are taxed separately for each individual in a family, and capital income is taxed on a base defined by the sum of the incomes of a married couple.

From 1980 the tax schedule for the income tax is partly indexed and contains some rules for a ceiling on both marginal tax rates and average tax rates. Table 9-5 presents part of the income-tax schedule. The concept of taxable income refers to the income after deduction of interest-rate expenditures (but with an imputed income for earner-occupied houses added) and deduction of expenditures for work journeys and so forth. The progressive state tax is added to the proportional local-authority tax in the table. The rate of the latter tax is assumed to be 30 percent which seems average for 1981.

Table 9-5
1981 Income-Tax Schedule

Taxable Income		Total Tax	Average Tax Rate	Marginal Tax Rate
Swedish Kronas	U.S. Dollars	SEK	(percent)	(percent)
25,000	5,810	5,576	22.3	32
50,000	11,625	14,248	27.7	44
75,000	17,440	27,670	34.8	69
100,000	23,255	43,288	43.2	74
125,000	29,070	62,500	50.0	78
150,000	34,880	81,440	54.3	80
200,000	46,510	121,840	60.9	85
300,000	69,765	206,840	68.9	85

It should be remembered that payroll tax is added to the taxable income. Disregarding interest-rate deductions, and so forth, one finds that a taxable wage income of 100,000 Swedish kronas corresponds to a gross salary before all taxes of about 125,000 SEK (equal to $29,000 U.S. currency). The total average tax rate will then be 70 percent and the marginal tax rate applied to the gross salary 82 percent (the payroll tax decreases above a limit of about 125,000 crowns). With this tax schedule, full-time employed skilled workers and professionals will have marginal tax rates of 70 percent and above.

The VAT for most goods is 23.5 percent. It is somewhat lower for construction, and some personal services are exempted as well as, for example, daily papers. Services produced by the local authorities are also exempted. With the present level of the VAT this has created some distortion problems as, for example, a hospital will find internally produced cleaning or laundry services cheaper than services bought externally from the private sector (which pays the VAT). The VAT expressed as a share of the GDP was about 8 percent in 1979, and the share of the total private consumption was slightly above 15 percent. Other indirect taxes come mostly from alcohol and tobacco, but even charter travels abroad have recently become a new tax source. In total, non-VAT indirect taxes will be about 10 percent of private consumption, though heavily concentrated on a few items.

Corporations are taxed twice in the sense that new profits before dividends but after deduction of interest rates, depreciations, and a number of specific deductions are taxed with a tax rate of about 55 percent. Dividends are then taxed as capital income added to the wage income for the stockholder.

This is not the place to discuss further the construction of different specific taxes such as inheritance taxes or capital-gains taxes. Only a few remarks are necessary. In contrast to the U.S. or British situation, the main source of income for the local authorities is the proportional income tax (plus transfers from central government). Rates on property do not exist. However, fixed property is given an imputed value added to other incomes. The level of the imputed income is 1 to 2 percent of the market value.

Corporate tax gives a very small fiscal revenue, mainly due to the fact of a sophisticated system of deductions. The total revenue is 1 percent of GDP. Most of the deductions were introduced in order to give different incentives for investment or research. This has resulted in a situation in which many companies have untaxed reserves of the same size as the equity capital.

It goes without saying that the tax system has become increasingly more complicated as the general level of taxation has increased. The first and basic rules are the tax schedules with the high tax rates. It has been obvious that these high tax rates will create a number of negative incentive effects. The second set of rules, therefore, allows a number of deductions, for example, for corporations or for savings on special accounts up to a limit for individual income earners. In order to prevent misuse, a third set of rules tries to counteract the second set of rules. This holds especially true for small business where the risk of tax avoidance and tax evasion is regarded as greatest. Last year these rules were supplemented with a general clause against tax avoidance.

One very obvious effect of the tax system is that all aspects of tax planning are among the most profitable private activities. This holds true for individual income earners as well as for corporations of all sizes. This means that considerable resources and ingenuity is diverted into tax planning and optimizing different decisions according to the net result after taxes. Some of the most striking examples will be found in the way in which portfolios are composed. One rather easy way to decrease the present tax level and perhaps indefinitely postpone taxes is to have assets with low nominal rates of return but with values following the price level (fixed property, shares) and to finance these assets by borrowing in nominal loans with deductible interest rates. The increases in nominal values will then only be taxed at a sale with a much lower capital-gains tax (capital gains on fixed property are calculated partly on an index-linked basis). With inflation increasing and with nominal rates of interest lagging somewhat behind, tax planning of this type has been increasingly widespread, especially among high-income earners with a possibility of financing interest payments and amortizations with new mortgage loans.

The Effects on Work Efforts

During the 1970s it was possible to observe an annual decline of 0.7 percent in the total number of hours worked at the same time as employment grew at 0.7 percent per year. A considerable decrease in the average number of working hours per employed person thus occurred. In 1979 the average was 1440 hours per year per employed worker. In comparison forty-six weeks with a 40-hour week would result in 1840 hours.) Behind this decrease are a multitude of different factors.

The labor market participation of men is decreasing at the same time as the participation of women is increasing. Deindustrialization is probably one important factor behind the decrease in male participation, and this decrease is facilitated by the generous system for early retirement pensions or part-time pensions. At the same time the heavy increase in employment in the public sector (health care, day-care centers, long-term care, and retirement homes) has increased demand for women workers. The increased female participation was also facilitated by a number of tax reforms in the late 1960s and in 1970 when incomes of married couples were taxed separately instead of being taxed as one income, which in general decreased marginal tax rates for the female part of the family. It is also reasonable to assume that the net result of taxes and increased benefits might be quite favorable for women starting part-time work as they will pay a rather low tax and at the same time qualify for paid maternity leaves, sickness payments, and unemployment benefits and acquire pension rights in the supplementary pension system.

With marginal tax rates normally being around 80 percent for professionals and 60 to 70 percent for skilled workers, incentives for overtime work or extra work have obviously become very small. For the correct decision between an extra hour of taxed work and an extra hour of leisure or do-it-yourself work, the correct calculation must be based on the total marginal effect of all taxes and income-related benefits. Although the correct calculation might be quite difficult and surrounded with uncertainty, it seems obvious that a learning process is going on and that the disincentive effects will grow even at unchanged tax levels as more and more individuals learn how to optimize their behavior.

To take a simple example: A worker with a marginal productivity equal to 100 SEK per hour, which is also assumed to be his gross wage rate (the wage cost to the employer), will first pay about 26 percent as a payroll tax (hidden in the sense that it is paid by the employer and never explicitly shown to the employee). He will then end up with 74 SEK before income tax. With a marginal tax rate of the ordinary income tax of 65 percent, he will earn as a net wage 26 crowns. If he is entitled to income-related housing and children allowances, these are decreased by up to 24 percent of taxable income, that is, the income after payroll taxes. His total marginal tax-increase-and-benefit-decrease rate might thus be 89 percent, and he will be left with 8 SEK in his pocket. If he is lucky (or perhaps unlucky) enough to have the children in a municipal day-care center with income-related fees, his total marginal rate might even exceed 100 percent. If one assumes that he gets no income-related social benefits or pay no income-related fees, of his 26 crowns 20 percent will be paid in VAT. Thus by producing commodities at a factor value of 100 SEK he will in the most favorable case be able to buy products or services of a factor value of 21 SEK. In the less favorable cases his increase in commodities will be completely insignificant or even negative. If the alternative is to produce the commodities by do-it-yourself activities (repairing the house or the car, making one's own meals instead of going to restaurant, and so forth), it suffices that his own productivity is about one-fifth of that of a skilled worker, and do-it-your-self work will still be a preferred alternative.

One would thus expect a large hidden or black sector of the economy in Sweden. Although evidence for very obvious reasons is scarce, the pattern of the Swedish hidden economy seems to be somewhat different than what has been assumed for countries like the United States or Italy. The pure criminal sector is probably rather small. A recent estimate of the total sales value of narcotic drugs showed a figure of 2 percent of GDP. Betting is legalized, but is is a state monopoly. Other estimates from interview surveys indicate that out of all transactions in the construction sector, about 5 percent of the transactions—mostly maintenance and repair—were not registered for tax purposes. Together with auto repair, this sector will probably be one in which one is most likely to find nontaxed transactions. (For a construction worker there will be a delicate cal-culation to find his optimal allocation between white and black work as work in the taxed sector is necessary to create some of the benefits of the social-welfare system and keep the investigations of the tax authorities at a low level.) The barter economy and nonregistered sector obviously exist, but it would be dangerous to assume that they play a large role except for some service sectors (including smaller restaurants).

By ad hoc observations one might imagine that the do-it-yourself sector and consumption-on-the-job or nontaxed fringe benefits play a more significant role as individual adjustments to high marginal rates. The Swedish skill structure is favorable for a lot of do-it-yourself activities like repairing or even building one's own house or summer cottage as most men are trained in simple carpentry work, and so forth. Few Swedish families would go to a restaurant for a Sunday dinner and pay with taxed money as the home production alternative is so favorable. The boom in owner-occupied houses and summer cottages during the 1970s might thus partly be explained by the fact that these sectors are tax sanctuaries. (High inflation, somewhat lower nominal interest rates, and tax-deductible interest rates are also a part of this story. Indirect observations of these increasing do-it-yourself activities show that sectors for private services which are substitutes for home production are declining sectors, for example, laundry services, barber services, and restaurant and hotel services for private consumption.

As has already been indicated there was a significant decrease in the growth of labor productivity in all sections between the 1960s and the 1970s. For some of the fast-growing public sectors there are even indications of a substantial de-crease in the absolute level of labor productivity. One factor that probably is highly related to the marginal tax rates and the social-welfare system is an in-creasing degree of absenteeism. Actual working hours are shortened by increas-ing part-time work and by increases in sickness leave, maternal (and even patern-al) leaves paid by social insurance or public employers, leaves for taking care of sick children paid by the sickness insurance, and so forth.

New laws were passed during the 1970s increasing the possibilities for per-forming trade-union work during paid working hours and allowing leaves for further education. It is not an extreme case when hospitals have more than two persons employed for each full-time position to compensate for all kinds of absence. The result of increasing planned or unplanned absences from work is a disorganization in routines and increasing demands for spending more time in transferring information to all employees. New laws regulating work environ-ments have had similar effects as they put a ceiling on the maximum number of hours of consecutive work and allow for breaks. Another factor was a new law on decision participation which is also regarded as time consuming since the information demand of all employees increases.

One could say that the labor force has become increasingly more skilled in choosing optimal working time with regard to taxes and benefits. As a general principle it seems that the optimal behavior is to have an employment contract, which means an indefinite employment according to the law on secure employment enacted in 1973. With this safe base the next optimization problem is to choose the hours worked during the year and the time spent on different social-benefit schemes. The optimum seems to lie below full working time for most groups. (As a far from extreme example, if a university professor takes one extra month of leave—preferably during semester time with a burden of lecturing—the loss of net income will be of the order of $550. (The gross salary cost for the university is for the same month $3,900.) It would be rather easy to compensate for this loss by do-it-yourself work or just by being a more informed consumer or enjoying the increased leisure.

One way of compensating workers without paying tax is to improve working conditions or increase fringe benefits. Some of the more obvious fringe benefits such as cars payed by the firm and expense accounts for entertaining customers (and oneself) have recently been heavily restricted by the tax authorities. However, there are always loopholes and imagination is for good reasons better on the taxpayers' side than on the tax authority's. Office standards are generally higher in Sweden than in the United States for comparable groups. A carpet on the floor is tax deductible for the firm but can hardly be taxed as income or consumption for the employee or consumer. (As the VAT system is constructed it is even free of VAT.) The growing interest in better work environments on all levels might have a very rational and simple explanation in the increasing marginal tax rates. If firms find it expensive to compete with wage conditions, untaxed fringe benefits in a very broad sense might be an attractive alternative to attract labor.

Conferences—often combined with journeys even abroad—belong to a booming sector, barely disguised as training but often with a considerable consumption element. In the statistics most of these fringe benefits and improved working environments are measured as input into production and not as a part of the value added or its salary component. An increase in the level of fringe benefits is thus automatically registered as a decrease in productivity. It is thus not unreasonable to conceive that parts of the decrease in productivity growth are actually a hidden shift from taxable income to different kinds of fringe benefits.

Until now the discussion has mainly centered around some of the short-term effects of the high marginal tax rates. Incentives for making careers and for education are also affected. Although hard data are not available, the general impression from both the private and the public sector is that employees have become less career oriented. A career is partly an investment in human capital: one is not paid immediately but at a later stage for the extra hard work. The analogy with education and training is obvious. The outcome of the extra efforts are taxed by the marginal tax rates and the private return might thus be small compared with the social return or the return to the employer. The declining recruitment at universities, especially for research studies, is one indication of these long-term effects and costs of high marginal tax rates. Firms complain about the difficulties of recruiting people at management level. (With the changes described in this chapter one might also assume that the equilibrium wage for top management would have to increase because of the tougher situation with increased worker's participation.) One way of evading the high marginal tax rates practiced in both the private and the public sectors for example, for ministers or members of parliament—is that of combining a moderate salary with very good pension conditions allowing for an early retirement or pension rights long before the age of sixty-five.

Effects on Savings and Capital Formation

The dominating motive for individual and voluntary wealth formation in a market economy is to get a more even distribution of consumption over the complete life cycle. A typical individual will have a gainful employment during forty to fifty years, but he will today expect to live ten to fifteen years after the age of sixty-five. Considering the risks of death before the age of sixty-five and a somewhat lower consumption at a higher age, an individual would have to save 20 to 25 percent of his labor income in order to get a reasonable level of consumption after the age of sixty-five. If one also considers consumption of health care, the savings requirement might be even higher. At present about 50 percent of all health care is spent on the 15 percent of the population above the age of sixty-five.

It should be observed that the Swedish population has a larger share of individuals above the age of sixty-five then the United States. Much of what is a cradle-to-grave redistribution program is then heavily concentrated at the grave part of the life cycle: basic pension, supplementary pension, special housing benefits, municipal care and homes for the retired, and as was stated above, a large share of the total health-care bill.

The market solution to the problem of redistributing incomes and consumption over the life cycle is a system of pension insurance, which can be combined with different types of health- and disability-insurance systems. A pension-insurance system is based on private savings and funds. The total volume of financial claims are determined by the number of individuals times the average assets. Each individual tries to build up assets which attain their maximum value when the pension period starts.

The Swedish solution—which is also the political solution—is a pay-as-you-go system. The present working generation transfers a part of its income to the retired and hopes that the next generation will show the same kind of benevolence. It is very close to the principle of a chain letter. No savings and no funds are in principle necessary. This chain-letter technique is applied to all the programs mentioned earlier with some small exceptions. When the supplementary pension system started in 1960, the fees were higher than paid-out pensions, and a deliberate element of forced collective savings was introduced to compensate for the reduction of savings in the previous dominating private systems.

The general rule of the supplementary pension scheme is that every person will receive 65 percent of an average of his previous labor income (measured as an average of the best fifteen years.) To get full supplementary pension in addition to the basic pension, which is equal for everybody regardless of previous income, it is, however, necessary to qualify during twenty years. The first individuals with full pension rights thus appeared in 1980. The qualification period will successively be brought up to thirty years.

This indicates another political and nonmarket feature with the pay-as-you-go systems. The first generation had a lower qualification time and paid less fees than the next generation. They were also a substantial part of the electorate in the referendum in 1957 when the system was approved. There is a tendency that with a pay-as-you-go system there will always be a majority of winners as the losers have not even reached voting age or are not fully aware of the debts that are put on them. (They can, of course, also hope to shift the burden to a still later generation.) A good example of this general principle occurred in 1975 when the pension age was decreased from sixty-seven to sixty-five years: the benefits were concentrated on a small but recognizable group while the costs were spread out and disguised in a general hidden payroll tax.

The present fund, based on forced collective savings, is now of the size that without new premiums it could pay out the pension claims of the present retired population during eight to ten years. It should also be mentioned that the introduction of the supplementary pension scheme probably increased mobility of labor in comparison with the small enterprise-based schemes that existed previously for blue-collar workers. White-collar workers were previously and are still eligible for some supplementary benefits relying on a nationwide scheme with transferability.

The main conclusion here is that the pay-as-you-go system eliminated one of the most important motives behind individual wealth accumulation. Savings decisions were thus made into a collective decision with forced savings and with government as the final owner of the financial assets. Although the pension fund is small in comparison with potential pension claims, it is still a giant in the financial market. In 1979 the gross financial assets excluding the value of the collective pension-insurance claims of private households were 320 billion SEK, and after debts of 245 billion SEK (mostly for owner-occupied houses), the private household had net assets of 75 billion SEK. (GDP during the same year was 435 billion SEK.) The value of the government supplementary pension fund was at the same time 150 billion SEK.

The other social-welfare programs have probably had similar effects. No private household needs to accumulate wealth for the education of the children (which is managed by government grants and loans systems) or to have a reserve in case of illness as health care is provided by the counties with no out-of-pocket costs, and sick pay and disability pensions are parts of the social-welfare system.

Added disincentives are the low or negative rates of return on financial savings with the combination of high marginal tax rates and high inflation hardly compensated by nominal interest rates. For retired persons a financial wealth might even be a disaster as some benefits to retired persons are decreased by 5 SEK for each 100 SEK they have as tax-assessed wealth. It is thus no surprise that financial savings in the household sector (disregarding the still existing private supplementary but collectively negotiated pension schemes) are negative or very close to zero. In 1979 the savings ratio of disposable income was -0.7 percent, and the last time the ratio was positive was in 1974 (+0.2 percent). That year was, however, a year of high unexpected wage rises.

Savings in owner-occupied houses have been positive during the last decade, amounting to about 5 percent of disposable income. This is hardly a surprise if one takes into consideration the beneficial tax situation for owners of private houses. At certain marginal tax rates many households will experience an enormous difference in costs between renting and owning. A typical new owner-occupied house will cost about five hundred thousand SEK. With mortgages up to 90 percent of the value and with government interest subsidies, the interest payments will be about thirty thousand SEK per year. The inputed income for taxation will be about ten thousand SEK, and twenty thousand SEK will thus be tax deductible. With 70 percent marginal tax rate the net nominal interest payments will be sixteen thousand SEK compared with a nominal increase in value of the house of fifty thousand to sixty thousand SEK per year at present inflation rates. The net cost will thus be minus thirty-five thousand SEK compared with the renting costs of a comparable flat of about thirty thousand SEK per year, of which one-half may be heating, maintenance, and repair costs. In the owner-occupied house much of the maintenance will be performed as do-it-yourself work or bought in the untaxed black sector. A study of the market for owner-occupied houses or other kinds of fixed assets will demonstrate many good examples of how to survive in an inflationary economy with extreme marginal rates of taxation. All political parties are also reluctant about limiting this sanctuary of privileges for the upper and the middle classes.

The main conclusion is thus that the creation of the welfare state has created a number of disincentives for private-wealth accumulation which has led to a collectivization of savings decisions and enforced savings through the tax system. It has been a shift in the rules of the game. In its first phase the supplementary pension fund was intended as a way of financing investments in housing and industry. The legal independence of the fund was a deliberate feature to underline the intention to compensate for the loss of private savings. During the last years with increasing government deficits the fund has been regarded much more as a comfortable way of financing the deficits. The investment ratio has also fallen during the 1970s from 22 to 20 percent of GDP, and industrial investments are now at the same level (in real value terms) as in 1970 but with investments in government-owned firms heavily increasing.

A typical feature of the welfare state is that almost no important group is depending on a higher return on capital: pensioners have their contracts with the next generations of taxpayers, universities and research foundations are tax financed, and parents have no need to pay for the education of their children. The remaining groups (some renters and a few more entrepreneurs) are too small to play any significant role in the political arena. This also results in a social situation in which the countervailing powers against excessive wage increases are suppressed—especially in a situation in which devaluations belong to rules of the game. A low real rate of return on the supplementary pension fund does not hurt the present generation of retired; the only consequence will be a rise in future payroll taxes. A further consequence is also that the political resistance against government intervention in the credit markets becomes small. Organized groups such as houseowners and farmers are winners in a system in which nominal interest rates are regulated down to low levels. Finally, the welfare state hurts some of the basic mechanisms of a capitalistic market economy, for example, the functioning of the market for equity capital. In the Swedish economy it is difficult to find a significant group that will be hurt as wealth owners if the value of stocks in private corporations just vanish.

Some Conclusions

The development outlined in this chapter is a history of fundamental changes in *institutions* and *contract structure*. The main tendency is an increase of the area of political decision making and a corresponding decrease of the market sector and the area for decisions based on voluntary exchange. Although a change in the political government occurred in 1976, no corresponding change seems to have developed in the actual policy. On the contrary, since 1976 government interference in the industrial sector has made a quantum jump with large-scale nationalizations. The social sectors have been growing at a higher pace than ever. Government deficit spending has for the first time in modern history become a serious problem. Contracts in the labor market depend more on trade-union negotiation than ever before. A last step in the destruction of the market system of voluntary exchange will now be discussed with probably a majority proposal to establish trade-union-dominated wage-earners' funds which will become the main owners of equity capital.

Biological scientists often put forward the hypothesis that the human genetic structure contains a death gene limiting human life to about 90 to 100 years with an average of fifty cell divisions. A study of the emergence of the Swedish welfare state suggests a simple analogy: irrespective of the political color of the government there has been a long-term tendency to substitute political institutions for market-oriented institutions. Sweden seems now to be very close to the end point of a market-economy system with government spending and regulations dominating the allocation and the distribution processes. Is it possible that the capitalistic system contains its own death gene when a large part of the prosperity and individual freedom created by the market system is devoted to annihilating the system itself?

Note

1. Public corporations such as railways, shipyards, and so forth, are excluded in this definition of the public sector except that losses in public enterprises are regarded as subsidies and accounted as transfers to the private sector.

Index

List of Contributors

James M. Buchanan, university professor, Virginia Polytechnic Institute and State University

R.M. Hartwell, professor of economics, Oxford University

F.A. von Hayek, Nobel Prize winner in economics, University of Freiburg

Peter F. Koslowski, assistant professor of philosophy, University of Munich

Karl-Dieter Opp, professor of sociology, University of Hamburg

Ingemar Ståhl, professor of economics, University of Lund

Viktor Vanberg, assistant professor, University of Munster

About the Editor

Svetozar Pejovich is professor of economics and the director of the Center of Education and Research in Free Enterprise at Texas A&M University. He is an adjunct scholar at the Heritage Foundation and a member of the editorial boards of the *Review of Social Economy, Modern Age,* and the Fisher Institute. He has published scholarly books and articles in the United States, Germany, Switzerland, Sweden, Austria, and Italy.

DATE DUE

Jan. 30 1984			